D0036968

We are grateful

to the households in the Christian Renewal Center at the College of Steubenville
and to the Franciscan Friars for their loving support and encouragement;

to Kevin Ranaghan, Ph.D. for his generous and competent assistance;

and, especially, to Fr. Augustine Donegan, T.O.R., theologian and brother, to whom this book is dedicated.

That very same day, two of them were on their way to a village called Emmaus, seven miles from Jerusalem, and they were talking together about all that had happened. Now as they talked this over, Jesus himself came up and walked by their side; but something prevented them from recognizing him. He said to them, "What matters are you discussing as you walk along?" They stopped short, their faces downcast.

Then one of them, called Cleopas, answered him, "You must be the only person staying in Jerusalem who does not know the things that have been happening there these last few days." "What things?" he asked. "All about Jesus of Nazareth" they answered "who proved he was a great prophet by the things he said and did in the sight of God and of the whole people; and how our chief priests and our leaders handed him over to be sentenced to death, and had him crucified. Our own hope had been that he would be the one to set Israel free. And this is not all: two whole days have gone by since it all happened; and some women from our group have astounded us: they went to the tomb in the early morning, and when they did not find the body, they came back to tell us they had seen a vision of angels who declared he was alive. Some of our friends went to the tomb and found everything exactly as the women had reported, but of him they saw nothing."

Then he said to them, "You foolish men! So slow to believe the full message of the prophets! Was it not ordained that the Christ should suffer and so enter into his glory?" Then, starting with Moses and going through all the prophets, he explained to them the passages throughout the scriptures that were about himself.

When they drew near to the village to which they were going, he made as if to go on; but they pressed him to stay with them. "It is nearly evening" they said "and the day is almost over." So he went in to stay with them. Now while he was with them at table, he took the bread and said the blessing; then he broke it and handed it to them. AND THEIR EYES WERE OPENED and they recognized him; but he had vanished from their sight. Then they said to each other, "Did not our hearts burn within us as he talked to us on the road and explained the scriptures to us?"

They set out that instant and returned to Jerusalem. There they found the Eleven assembled together with their companions, who said to them, "Yes, it is true. The Lord has risen and has appeared to Simon." Then they told their story of what had happened on the road and how they had recognized him at the breaking of bread.

(Luke 24:13-35, Jerusalem Bible)

CONTENTS

PREFACE

Charismatic Renewal appears in the world especially within the domain of prayer groups, and within the Renewal one is often stopped by that which surprises the imagination, that which seems new or at least extraordinary. The trees need not hide the forest! The grace of charismatic renewal moves eminently and primarily through the avenues of grace which are the sacraments. The outstanding merit of this book is the manner in which it calls attention to the renewed presence of the Holy Spirit in the very heart of the sacramental life of the Church. The book emphasizes also the fact that each sacrament is a personal encounter with Jesus. In this manner, the sacraments are put in their true perspective: "The Lord still lives today, with a Power in the service of an immense Love." That same power that Jesus exhibited in days past is present among us if we can but recognize it. "And their eyes were opened . . ." remains a scene from the Gospel present even today: in one way or another we are all disciples on the road to Emmaus—confused men and women in need of Someone to explain the Scriptures to us and Someone to come to sit at our table.

Michael Scanlan and his collaborator [Ann Thérèse Shields, R.S.M.] speak with a faith-filled language, with simplicity, with a wise and precise pastoral message. It is a message accesible to their readers; it is a message filled with the compassion of the Lord for all.

We have warmly appreciated their pages. A sincere wish is that charismatic renewal might aid in revitalizing each of our seven sacraments and then that it might be felt in our parish liturgical celebrations as a new start, a new spring. This book gives us a foretaste of that spring.

Cardinal L.J. Suenens
Archbishop, Malines-Brussels

1

An Introduction: Relics and Ritual

"The sacraments? Dead." "They mean nothing." "They have little significance for me, but I wish they did." "Something the Catholic Church does." "So many times they seem more like social customs—something to be done because it's proper, like Baptism, First Communion, Marriage." "I participated because it made my parents proud of me." "It was kind of exciting in grade school when you were getting ready to receive one of the sacraments. We felt special but after a while it wore off, and the sacraments just became something you did because you were Catholic." "Sacraments frightened me. I felt I wasn't good enough." "It's routine. I know God gives me grace because that's what we were taught, but I don't experience it and somehow I think I should." "I only 'did it' because everyone else did and I was in Catholic school. It was part of the school schedule and expected." "I know God is present but somehow I've always felt I had to measure up in some way before I could receive him in the sacrament. That's exhausting and sometimes I feel guilty."

These are typical expressions of the place the sacraments have had in the lives of many Catholics. Of course, some persons testify to *a* significant experience in one or another sacrament. However, this experience is seen either as a singular, rarely repeatable encounter with God or as a frequent life-giving encounter within *one* sacrament. In our experience,

Catholics normally do not see the sacraments as the *usual* way Jesus wishes to constantly meet and deepen his relationship with his people in a creative, dynamic, and transforming process. Rarely do Catholics realize that each encounter in any sacrament has the power to change their lives for the better.

Four years ago, I (Fr. M.) wrote a booklet, *The Power in Penance* (Ave Maria Press, 1972), which discussed a new approach to the sacrament of Penance. The booklet was based on my experience of life-changing power being released in confessions. I detailed the ways in which priest and penitent could respond to the movement of the Holy Spirit in the sacrament.

The response to the book overwhelmed me. About 100 priests wrote to tell me that their new pastoral approach to the sacrament was bearing fruit. An even larger number of penitents informed me that they had received healings and new freedom through this new approach to the sacrament.

During the years since *The Power in Penance* appeared, I have come to see that there is a general approach to all the sacraments that brings forth life-changing power. I believe that Catholics and other Christians can know a personal, powerful encounter with Jesus in each sacramental celebration. I believe this will happen to a very limited extent if we only learn about the sacraments and their new rites. Of course we need to appreciate the value in Vatican II's teaching on the sacraments and we need to study the revised rites of the sacraments. But, fundamentally, we need to discover the sacraments for ourselves as individuals and as members of a worshipping community, much as the early Church led by the Holy Spirit first discovered the sacraments in its midst. We may be familiar with the sacraments; we may receive them frequently. This does not mean that we really know them as God would have us know them.

An experience I had 10 years ago will illustrate this. Traditionally, Franciscans hold a novena in preparation for the

Feast of Saint Francis on October 4. At The College of Steubenville, our evening novena included a time of reverencing a first-class relic of Saint Francis. Reverencing consisted of kissing the glass top of the case which held the relic. In the wave of post-Vatican II liturgical reforms, many of us had become restless with our traditional novena format. Nevertheless, we continued in the same manner and no one suggested any changes. Then one night in the middle of the 1966 novena, while the congregation was lined up to reverence the relic, a small child's voice rang out throughout the chapel. His words penetrated everyone present as he said, "Mummy, can I smell it too?" We suddenly realized that we were finding no more meaning in this form of reverencing than the child found. No one attempted to explain what we were doing. The child's mother quieted him and we continued mechanically through the ritual. But that was the last night that kissing the relic was part of our novena. We unanimously agreed to drop it. We then talked about revising the novena format to induce a more prayerful atmosphere.

In this book we attempt to perform the function of the child and call attention to what isn't working in the sacraments. We do this in order to show what can work.

Since we became involved in the charismatic renewal, we have experienced new power in the sacraments, best described for us as sacraments coming alive. We have investigated the experience of others and have concluded that our personal insights are valid. Through a survey of 600 priests who attended the First National Conference for Priests on Charismatic Renewal at The College of Steubenville in June 1975, and through interviews with a cross-section of lay people, we conclude that sacraments can be life-changing events for all believers. We believe that priests and lay persons need not have special holiness or advanced theological understanding in order to experience sacraments this way. Rather, every person who believes in the lordship of Jesus Christ can encounter Jesus in a personal life-changing way through the sacraments.

This book offers a very limited treatment of sacraments. We do not intend to review the whole theology of each sacrament. We do not even intend to investigate the meaning of the liturgical changes flowing from the Second Vatican Council.

What we do intend is to focus simply on what we have found to be most life-giving and transforming in our experience of the sacraments. In this way we hope that the knowledge we have gained will not be lost in the midst of other essential but, nevertheless, for our purposes, secondary considerations.

All the material we have discerned and explored together. However, there are certain areas where our experience has given us different perspectives. When this occurs, the pronoun "I" is used, with the author identified in parentheses.

We offer, then, the following pages not as definitive material but rather as a charting of what we believe to be vital direction for all of God's people who hunger for deeper spiritual nourishment in the sacraments.

2

An Overview of the Sacraments

We are a "meeting" generation. So frequently, whatever our state in life, we are called to participate in gatherings of either an academic, business, religious, or civic community nature. As a result we have become quick to characterize meetings by such expressions as "that was deadly" or "the meeting was really alive tonight." These expressions characterize the spirit of the meeting. They evaluate a number of things for us: (a) how meaningful the encounter was among the persons present; (b) how directly the issues were handled; and (c) the nature of the response among the participants. Similarly, we can speak about personal appointments which drag, and those which excite and stimulate. Such characterizations obviously refer to the personal, subjective response of those involved. It is also important to note that, apart from subjective reactions, important transactions can and often do take place even during the deadest of meetings.

With this frequent personal experience in mind, let us take an introductory glance at the sacraments.

Sacraments are encounters with Jesus. These encounters pledge grace* to us just as if we had met Jesus on the roads of

*If we understand sacraments as encounters, we will understand grace rightly. We often view grace in a quantitative way, as a bank account or a storehouse to be added to and hoarded until the

Galilee. If we had met Jesus in biblical times, we would have met a Jesus who was preaching good news, teaching the truth about men's lives, healing, casting out evil, performing miracles, and calling people into a community of disciples. Our lives would certainly have been graced by such a meeting.

Of course, such an encounter would not necessarily be a subjectively important experience for us. While it is obvious that the more we were aware of who Jesus was and what power he possessed, the more alive we would have been to the encounter, it is also obvious that it would have been possible to encounter Jesus simply as a fellow traveler who was of no importance to us. It would have been possible to meet him without the meeting having any vitality.

In the same way, we can encounter Jesus in the sacraments with little attention to what is happening. We do receive new life in Baptism and a new presence of Jesus in the reception of the Eucharist. Yet, people often find such times of encounter empty and lacking in vitality. Those sacraments celebrated more frequently, such as Penance and the Eucharist, are naturally far more susceptible to becoming mechanical even if the external rite is rich in meaning. No one doubts the effect of the consecration or the absolution. Some important things do happen. But many *subjective* things do not happen. The participants in the sacraments are not aware of the presence of Jesus; they are not open to an encounter that could change the way they live; they do not respond prayerfully; they do not commit themselves to one another and to the Lord. They are passive participants receiving the minimum benefits of the occasion and sensing the impotence of what they know to be a sacred moment.

---

moment of death. Instead, grace flows from our encounter with Jesus. It is God favoring us, blessing us, touching us, acting toward us in a loving, saving way. Grace is a dynamic living relationship whereby we mysteriously share in the life of God.

Thus, there is an almost universal dissatisfaction with the present experience of the sacraments. This is true despite the evident improvements through the revised rites since Vatican II.

Obviously there are exceptions to the situation as we have described it. Many parishes in the United States offer excellent adult and parent-child preparation programs for Baptism, Penance, Eucharist, and Confirmation. Likewise, many parishes have developed and adopted the Pre-Cana series and encouraged participation in Engaged and Marriage Encounter programs as essential to the preparation for and the growth of good marriages. Through their parish councils or interested individuals, some parishes have developed excellent seminars in liturgical worship so that those gathered for sacramental celebrations may more deeply understand what it is to worship as the body of Christ. And finally, in each Catholic's life, there are memorable moments of sacramental experience. These are certainly vital signs of the fruit of Vatican II and of the dynamic presence of God's Spirit in dedicated laity, religious, deacons, and priests.

Nevertheless, it must still be admitted that the experience of deadness is more common today. Many people have the unspoken attitude that the sacraments are "something the Church does"—"they are what makes the Catholic Church Catholic." Baptism is seen as a "social" sacrament, an obligation imposed by the society of the Church. Parents seeking the best for their children conform to this practice of providing "the means to heaven" without a deep understanding of its spiritual significance for them and the child.

Penance is often experienced as a burden, something to be "gotten over with," at best a temporary reprieve from the effects of sin and guilt and fear. It often involves repeating the same sins and the same penance—an empty experience of reciting formulas to fulfill an Easter duty.

Confirmation is seen as making little or no sense since the one confirmed as a witness to the gospel does nothing differently in or out of the Church than before. To many being confirmed, there is a sense of "we let you in at Baptism," but now you have to prove yourself worthy by answering all the questions the Church sets before you through the Confirmation ritual.

The sacrament of Matrimony is often seen as a means to fulfill a social obligation and a way to receive God's blessing. But is the sacrament seen as enabling and supplying what is necessary to make the marriage itself really work?

Anointing of the Sick is still too often seen as a nice farewell sacrament providing the opportunity to get "things cleaned up." Rarely does anyone expect the sacrament to be a source of healing.

These statements are a synthesis of many comments gained from both lay people and religious. Obviously, heaviness and deadness in the sacraments are common experiences today.

And yet we have known the sacraments alive. We have had experiences with a baptismal liturgy which brought a parish congregation into a sense of oneness and led us to identify with the infant as our son. We have been at marriages where the sense of Jesus embracing his bride was as vivid as the embrace of the newlyweds. Either as celebrant or participant, we have experienced the Anointing of the Sick where the sense of healing was so overwhelming that we knew the sick person would recover. One time this occurred at a house of prayer where an elderly and ill sister asked for the sacrament so that she could get up and celebrate Easter. She was healed, got up, and stayed up for two years. For me (Fr. M.), the celebration of the sacrament of Penance has been my most frequent experience of new life. I have seen many penitents receive new hope, new courage, new love, new insights, and healings from the emotional traumas of past life.

Our experience is not yet the common experience in the Church. We have experienced many sacramental celebrations which lacked these signs of life, fewer than before we became involved in charismatic renewal, but still too many. We are convinced that the Father wants us to celebrate these sacraments not so much by external preparations, through liturgical committees, good music, specially chosen readings, lighting, colorful vestments, and well-prepared homilies. Though these are certainly important elements, they will not, of themselves, make the sacraments alive for the participants. Rather, the Father wants us to celebrate primarily by expecting to find Jesus there. Where we find Jesus, we find life and light and hope.

At the First National Conference for Priests on Charismatic Renewal at The College of Steubenville, Steubenville, Ohio in June 1975, 215 of the 600 priests present responded to a survey on the sacraments. More than one-half of the priests responding indicated that their people now experienced a new and deeper life in the sacrament of Penance; one-fourth expressed new life and healing in the Eucharist; almost one-third witnessed to physical, emotional, or spiritual healing through the Anointing of the Sick. Overall, a pastoral hope and excitement about the future of the sacraments was obvious throughout the conference.

These priests were indicating, in effect, that the sacraments had come alive for them and their people. It is equally true that while many other people hunger for God's life, desire it, and seek it in the sacraments, they do not have a clear understanding of what to expect, of what is possible.

Many of those with whom we spoke and interviewed and who acknowledged the heaviness and deadness in sacramental events also indicated this hunger and were able to articulate some of their hopes, their belief of what the sacraments are meant to be in the lives of all God's people. While they acknowledged that the full power of sacramental life is found in the heart of a worshipping community, that no sacramental event is simply a "God and me" experience, nevertheless they maintained, as do we, that a personal understanding and expectancy in the sacraments is important in order that God may more fully empower, love and heal us into whole, vitally alive members of the body of Jesus Christ. The following reflections then are a synthesis of the hunger, conviction, and actual experiences of many religious and lay persons.

In Baptism, an adult, or a child through his parents, by the power of the Spirit, rejects the kingdom of darkness as having any authority to rule his life. He accepts the kingdom of light and is consecrated and dedicated to the Lord. The sacrament empowers the individual to live and move in the victory of Jesus Christ, won for him on the cross. The community welcomes the person and pledges responsibility to incorporate him lovingly and supportively into the body of Jesus Christ.

In Confirmation, we accept responsibility to live in the body of Christ and to support it by those gifts God has given us. The Church confirms that those gifts are truly of the Spirit and empowers and calls us to use them for service. We are now witnesses of God's love and power in our lives. We can testify to it through our ministries, and the community of the Church pledges to support our growth.

In the Eucharist, we can expect to be healed each time we receive—healed physically, spiritually, and empowered to deal with those relationships and situations of that day with Jesus' wisdom and love and strength. We are given those gifts in his body and blood. As we consume his body, we are more able to see our place in it, our relationship to others in the body of Jesus Christ. We are also given understanding about how to deal with that knowledge in a practical way. Finally, through the Eucharist, we are drawn into deeper personal union with him who is Lord of our lives.

In Penance, we now know that to be holy is first to desire and experience forgiveness. The sacrament is a life-giving experience, not an act of condescension on the part of God. In God's healing presence, with the gifts given the confessor and penitent, we can discern the root of a sin, know that it can be destroyed and know that the pain can be healed by his power. Each time we are forgiven, we can know a new freedom to enter more deeply into our personal love relationship with Jesus. We are a new creation, transformed. We are never the same. We can expect to act and feel differently because in Penance areas of sin are healed and forgiven forever. We are free because Jesus desires our freedom and wholeness and life even more than we do.

In the Anointing of the Sick, we can experience in our need the most loving thing God desires to do for us. We *expect* that to happen to us and to those for whom we gather to pray as they receive the sacrament. We expect to see the sick restored to health; we expect to see deep peace in those who embrace God's will of redemptive suffering for them; we expect to see those called approach death with joy and total confidence. That is the power we know and can expect each time we participate in or witness the sacrament of Anointing of the Sick.

In Holy Orders, a person is called into a special order within the body of Christ. It is a uniquely holy position, for he is called by the community which has supported his gifts and life to be their intercessor and mediator before God, to offer sacrifice, to call forth adoration and praise. As that person has grown, the members of the Christian community recognize that they can place special confidence and trust in him, that his life is representative of them, and they desire that he stand, so to speak, between them and God. Through its bishop, the community seals that call and anoints him as priest forever. The community is again hereafter responsible for what it has nurtured, called forth, and confirmed. He who accepts that call is empowered by the sacrament to lay down his life for God's own.

In Matrimony, God anoints two people to be the sign, the tangible witness of the way he loves and is united to his Church. Two people make public their desire to lay down their lives for one another in love, to so be for the other that their love can encourage and support and be a sign of hope to the whole body. Their covenant, made public by the sacrament, is to become a reflection of God's covenant of love with his people. The sacrament so empowers them to give their lives to one another that they are made one. That physical and spiritual union is a concrete sign of God's desire to be one with his people. The community, which has nurtured the couple's lives and called forth their gifts, now confirms their love as a life-giving sign of hope and light to the community. The community desires that such a love be a permanent beacon to them and they support the couple to seal that union in the power of God. The sacrament also gives the couple power to bring forth in love and responsibility new lives for the Father's kingdom—lives the couple is empowered to nurture into mature and responsible freedom.

In this chapter, we have summarized the experiences of those who have experienced deadness in the sacraments and have now found life. Because of their experiences, they believe that the widespread hunger for new vitality in the sacraments can be satisfied through the action of the Risen Lord among his people. But how do we pass from death to life, from frustration to hope and expectancy? Obviously we cannot just decide the sacraments are dead and need to come alive. We must allow a process of transformation to take place whereby we encounter Jesus and come together as Church—to receive and celebrate the Life among us. In the next two chapters we

will develop the means by which that transformation can begin
to take place.

3

Church Alive

Sacraments will not come alive until The Sacrament is alive. The Sacrament is the Church. The seven sacraments flow from the one Sacrament, the Church.* For any particular celebration of the sacraments, the Church is that body of believers gathered together for the celebration. The extent to which that body of believers has not come alive to being Church limits the possibility of that particular sacramental celebration being alive. This point requires some explanation.

The world is populated by those who see themselves as unloved and alienated. But there are so few who seek this love from God. "Who will love me?" is the burning question; to reply "God" is not considered a responsible answer. God is not real, not personal enough. He can't be touched or seen, so how can he meet the need for love of millions of real people whose craving causes anxiety and loneliness which, in turn, give form to so many activities of their daily life? Indeed, for

*"The term 'sacrament' is here applied to the Church by analogy with the seven sacraments properly so called which are particular actions of Christ in and through the Church. The Church itself is a sort of 'general sacrament' since as the Constitution . . . explains, it is a 'sign and instrument' of the grace which unites men supernaturally to God and to one another." ("Dogmatic Constitution on the Church," footnote 3, p. 15, as cited in *The Documents of Vatican II*. Walter M. Abbott, S.J. (ed.). New York: The America Press, 1966.)

most Christians, God is still Yahweh of the Old Testament. He is the One who exists, the mighty God of power, the Holy One beyond man's reach. He is other than what is real and personal to man.

Yet Jesus revealed to us a different God—God who is family. He revealed a Father who loved his Son infinitely and who loves us as adopted sons and daughters. He revealed himself as the Word become flesh. He, in human body, with all the feelings of man, was also God. In Jesus we touch God—we can relate to him in a real, personal way. In Jesus, God identified his life with ours. God became present in flesh that could be seen and touched. When he was touched in faith, lives were changed. The woman with the hemorrhage said to herself, "If I can but touch the hem of his garment, I will be healed." So she struggled forward through the crowd, reached out and touched the hem. Immediately Jesus asked, "Who touched me?" The disciples did not understand. There was a pressing crowd all about, many people were touching him. But Jesus made it clear, "I felt power going out from me." Finally, the woman is identified and Jesus says to her, "Your faith has made you whole." The evangelists write that "all upon whom he laid his hands were healed." We can imagine the struggle to get to Jesus. Crowds followed him into the desert. He had to preach from Simon's boat because the crowds occupied all the room on the shore. The evangelists give us a picture of a Jesus besieged by the multitudes who would make him king. This is particularly true when he multiplies the loaves and fishes so that thousands of hungry followers might eat (Matt. 14:13-21).

But the man Jesus could touch so few men and women. He could barely come in contact with all the residents of his district. In view of the enormity of people's needs, it makes sense that Jesus would tell the apostles: "It is better for you that I go;" for then the Father would send the Spirit and the apostles would do even greater deeds than Jesus did. Yet this made no sense to the apostles. Jesus was the leader, the teacher, the healer, the miracle worker, their reason for life. How could they be anything but impoverished by his going? Yet Jesus knew the truth of the Spirit. Luke reflects this truth in the fifth chapter of his gospel when he writes: "One day Jesus was teaching and the Power of the Lord made him heal. . ." (Luke 5:17). Jesus knew that the power of healing was in the Spirit which was to be poured out on *all* mankind.

Jesus knew the Holy Spirit by whom he and the Father were bound together. Jesus knew the Holy Spirit was the embodied love of the Father for him and his love for the Father. He knew that the Father had given all things to him and that he in turn sought only to do the Father's will. He and the Father were totally given in love for the other. And that love so total, so completely expressed, is a person equal to both. This third person is the Holy Spirit. This Spirit, who functions to express the love of God, is the power of healing and saving love. Therefore, Jesus knew that through his death, resurrection, and glorification, this Spirit would be released for all men. Jesus knew that in this Spirit the disciples could reach out in healing love and touch many more people than Jesus could ever meet. Yet Jesus says to them that he will be with them all days, even to the consummation of the world. How will he be with them? Through the Holy Spirit, his Spirit, dwelling within them. They will be his Church. Just as Jesus was the sacrament of God, making God visible to men, so this body of men and women, the Church of Jesus, will be the sacrament of Jesus, making Jesus present to the whole world. And from the Church, Jesus will have special presence in word and sacraments.

With this background of how Jesus is present in the Church, we will now reflect on the concepts and responses which are key to our celebrating Church today.

Celebration of Church

In every sacrament, it is the Church celebrating through those members of the body present. The individual sacraments can only be celebrated to the extent that the first sacrament, the Church, is celebrated by those present. If the participants do not know the Spirit, they will not be able to celebrate as Church. To a great extent they will be onlookers or functionaries in a prescribed ritual. They will not be alive to who they are. The first sacrament, the Church, will not be acknowledged. Therefore it will not be celebrated, and therefore, the individual sacrament will lack vitality in its celebration.

How, then, do we celebrate the first sacrament, the Church? There can be many answers to this question. Certainly, whenever we act as members of the body of Jesus we are strengthening our ties to one another as Church. Doing the work of Jesus is an expression of the body of Jesus. Yet these answers are inadequate for the ordinary Christian who desires to celebrate as a Church member and to have the sacraments alive in his life.

The first step toward celebrating the first sacrament, the Church, is to realize that the kingdom of God is truly at hand and that therefore Jesus is reigning in our lives as Lord of that kingdom. If that is so, and we maintain that it is, then we must first examine what is meant by the proclamation, "The reign of God is at hand" and what is meant by the cry of Christians, "Jesus is Lord." In this way we can more fully understand in a practical way how we are to celebrate Church as the sacrament of Jesus.

The Kingdom of God

The "reign of God is at hand" is the primary pronouncement of the evangelists. Luke repeats this statement in variant forms 40 times. It is the proclamation of John the Baptist and of Jesus. Jesus instructs the twelve and the seventy-two to proclaim this message as he sends them forth. This message gives meaning to the signs and wonders, instructing the people that the healings and miracles are the signs of the kingdom at hand, here in their midst. God is now reigning as he promised he would. That pronouncement is just as true for us today as it was for the first disciples. Through the power of the Spirit, we see God overcoming sickness, blindness, deafness, oppression, ignorance, and all evil. Christian communities are springing up where the Beatitudes (Matt. 5) are developing into the normative values for daily living; where the young, many of whom have been born and raised amidst material prosperity, desire to sell what they have, give to the poor and dedicate their lives to the spreading of the good news; where old and young alike are learning to bear the cross of Jesus Christ with new power. God's reign is real and true. It is at hand, handy. You can reach out and touch it by reaching out and touching Jesus. Yes, Jesus has overcome the world. His kingdom *is* at hand.

This was news indeed 2000 years ago to a people who had been ruled by Assyrians, Babylonians, and Greeks, and were then under the reign of the Romans. In our day, whether we have suffered under tyrannical government or not, we have all known a time when something controlled and dictated our way of thinking and acting. Perhaps our own lives or the lives of those close to us have been ruled by materialism, drugs, or competition. It limited our freedom as sons and daughters of God and often destroyed our peace. Perhaps the desire for success reigned so strongly that we manipulated people and ideas to place ourselves in the limelight and to glory in the praise of others. Perhaps the lord of our lives was the vicious cycle of "keeping up with the Joneses" in material possessions which tore us with worry and debt.

We are all aware of the reign of drugs and alcohol which causes those so addicted to center their whole lives around their next fix or next drink. We are all aware of the reign of the kingdom of darkness in our cities through fraud, pornography, prostitution, and perversion. Everywhere we look we can see a heaviness that grips and presses on our spirit. In that burden, there is no doubt what reigns.

Jesus came to proclaim the good news that the *reign of God* is at hand. He embodied that good news as he healed the sick, exorcised demons, and preached. After the resurrection, Jesus reigned and reigns as Lord in the kingdom of God. He is the way to the kingdom, and he becomes the means for all people to have the reign of God be the reigning force in their lives. After the resurrection, the cry is no longer "The kingdom of God is at hand," but a refrain that expresses so much more—"Jesus is Lord." This means, in the fullest expression, that the kingdom of God is here and available to us, and that Jesus, whom we know, is reigning as Lord of that kingdom. Thus, "Jesus is Lord" has been the anthem of Christians through the centuries.

The Lordship of Jesus

But how do we arrive at the place where the kingdom is the ruling principle of our lives and where Jesus is the Lord? The apostle Paul is very precise: "No one can say Jesus is Lord except in the power of the Spirit." Now it is clear that Paul does not merely refer to the act of pronouncing the words "Jesus is Lord." What he means is that only in the power of the Holy Spirit can a person sufficiently know the lordship of

Jesus to proclaim it. Another way of saying it is that we can have the faith to know the lordship of Jesus only in the power of the Spirit. While this knowing or faith has a basis in objective reality, it goes beyond reason. Our faith in the lordship of Jesus goes deeper than belief in a rational truth, such as the distance and size of stars. Paul refers to an *immediate* truth: the truth that Jesus is lord of my life. When I proclaim Jesus as lord of my life, I proclaim that he is immediately involved in my life, that he orders my life as a lord supervises his servants, that he has a plan for my life within the overall plan of the kingdom of God, and that I can know and follow his guidance. This is a momentous statement. When it is an acknowledged truth in someone's life, it revolutionizes his way of thinking and acting. He begins to live with expectant faith.

Faith Response

Expectant faith is distinguished from dogmatic faith and quasi-providential faith.* Dogmatic faith is belief in principles, truths, and dogmas, and is expressed in creeds. Quasi-providential faith is faith in the divine providence of God to *ultimately* take care of everything. To have quasi-providential faith, it is sufficient to believe that God will reward the good, punish the evil, and see that justice is done in the end. It means that God is not necessarily involved in our personal lives, but that he sees all and will rectify and reward as warranted.

Expectant faith includes dogmatic and providential faith but goes further to proclaim that God is involved in every act. The Lord is Lord here and now, and his power is able to make a difference in each act. We therefore speak of the surprises of

*While true providential faith would expect God's providence to be active from moment to moment, providence is more often understood in a quasi sense: "quasi—having some resemblance, usually by possession of certain attributes." Webster

the Spirit. These surprises can be seen as interventions of God as long as we do not see them in what is traditionally known as a *deus ex machina* understanding of God. *Deus ex machina* (god from the stage machine) is a concept derived from the early Greek theater by which the gods directly intervened in the lives of men. They did so by being lowered into the human situation through a trap door high above the stage. When the need was met, the gods would be whisked up and out of the world of man. Expectant faith does not mean pulling God down into moment-to-moment affairs, but rather sees God's continual response through the constant presence of the Holy Spirit who infills the lives of Christians and gives direction to the Church.

Thus, as a Christian, through expectant faith, I can expect the Lord to be Lord in each event of my life. I can expect to know his guidance and power. He will not interfere with my free will; I will still sin and make unwise decisions. He will not take over or be present in a visible way; I must still struggle in faith to follow his lead. But I can *expect* his guidance and power to be present.

How do we reach this point? How do these words become more than pious phrases? How do we experience Jesus reigning in a personal way in our lives?

The answer involves a process where first we accept the truth that we are loved by God. In John 17, we read the early Church's understanding of Jesus' prayer for his disciples:

> I have given them the glory you gave me
> that they may be one, as we are one—
> I living in them, you living in me—
> that their unity may be complete.
> So shall the world know that you sent me,
> and that you loved them as you loved me.
> Father,

all those you gave me
I would have in my company
where I am,
to see this glory of mine
which is your gift to me,
because of the love you bore me before the world began.
Just Father,
the world has not known you,
but I have known you;
and these men have known that you sent me.
To them I have revealed your name,
and will continue to reveal it
so that your love for me may live in them,
and I may live in them.

(John 17:22-26)

Do we know what that means? Are we able to receive the truth of that word? I am loved in the same way that the Father loves his Son Jesus. That truth is so startling that we are tempted to reject it saying, "That couldn't be what is meant." But it is!

When this knowledge—that I (Sr. A.) was loved in the same way the Father loves the Son—began to penetrate my mind and heart, it affected my life in a radical way. I saw that such love was not measured or determined by my degree of un-worthiness. I began to see that that overwhelming love was a free gift which I was asked to accept. Isn't it what we most desire? Isn't someone loving and supporting and protecting us what we all seek for? And how often we turn to other things to compensate for our loneliness, our frustration, and pain. God extends to us in Jesus the gift of his love—a love which is constant, a love which will not be taken from us, a love we can base our lives on. We have the right by our free will to accept or reject that love.

My own experience has been that when we accept his love and genuinely surrender our lives, with all their dark and bitter and painful corners, we begin to know a presence and strength we never thought possible. God's Spirit, the love between the Father and Son, pours that love into our hearts and draws us into the beginnings of a deep and intimate union with the Father and Jesus. In the certainty of that love, we have the courage to face our sins, the areas of darkness in our lives. We know in the experience of that love his eternal, merciful forgiveness. We accept that we will never be worthy—we see our guilt and infidelity. But now, as never before, we are not condemned by that knowledge, weighed down and burdened by our sin. For we have experienced the love of the Father. We know the greatest proof of his love in his Son Jesus. Jesus is our Savior. He has freed us. The knowledge of our infidelity now only leads us to embrace Jesus more completely, to recognize his healing, redemptive love for us, to ask him to rule and direct our lives, and to lead us deeper into the freedom we are beginning to know. Here is true freedom, and we know it to the roots of our beings. By his healing love in the power of his Spirit, we desire him as Lord. We need him as Lord—we call out to him, "Jesus, be Lord! Be Lord over my life, my future, be Lord of my hopes and my talents, be Lord even over my sins and failings, be Lord of my emotions, my mind, be Lord of my life. Reign over me—for I know no harshness in your rule—I know only the convicting and consoling call to truth and freedom."

The truths I have expressed here only came to me gradually. However, each one was like a solid rock on which I could base my life and move more and more into the fullness of life God desires us all to share with him.

That is the surpassing power of his love in the Spirit. That is the transformation of love we can expect in our lives. In his love we can face the whole truth of our lives, however painful.

We can experience the truth of God's peace in our lives, and in that gift begin to know who he is and who we are. That truth shall make us free.

This kind of love provides a strong base to grow in expectant faith. No matter what daily situations may occur, no matter what life presents us, the certainty of God's love will assure us that we can honestly expect him to do the most loving thing in our lives. Anything else would be contrary to his nature. Even when our faith is most strongly tested we can still depend on and expect God's loving signs of new life in the midst of death, light in the face of darkness—that is the power of his resurrection and it is ours through the life of his Spirit.

Church Alive—Beginnings

This, then, is the starting point to celebrate Church. Christians are called to know the Spirit in this way and be able to proclaim, "Jesus is Lord."

This is what the apostle Paul means by proclaiming "Jesus is Lord." It is what a Christian means by saying "the kingdom of God is at hand." It is what happened on Pentecost when the disciples were changed from a group of followers banded together without their master to a band of witnesses going forth believing in the presence of their Lord and Master. In that faith, in that kingdom experience, we are able to gather together to celebrate Church as the visible sign that the Lord Jesus is living and reigning among us.

This is the experience that over 600,000 Catholics in the United States and thousands of other Christians throughout the world have had when they were baptized in the Holy Spirit or experienced the release of the power of the Spirit which was already present through the sacrament of Baptism. These Christians have asked Jesus to be Lord over their lives and to lead them by the power of the Holy Spirit. They have discovered new power to praise, new power to respond to the words of Scripture, and new ability to spend time in prayer. Other charismatic gifts, such as praying in tongues, prophecy, and healing, flow from this experience (see 1 Cor. 12-13; Eph. 4:11-16; Romans 12:3-13).

For our purposes, the most important thing that happens after being baptized in the Spirit is the growth of a desire to pray together with others. This leads to prayer meetings such as Paul describes in 1 Corinthians 12 and 13 (see 1 Cor. 14:26-33; Col. 3:16-18; Acts 2:46-47). Such prayer meetings are occurring today in the charismatic renewal. These meetings are marked by a sense of unity in the Spirit, strong praise, deep prayer, and the centrality of the Word of God. The meeting begins and continues under the explicit call to follow Jesus as Lord. The Christians gathered celebrate that they are in the Church, and for the time of prayer, they are the celebrating Church in that specific location. They have discovered that Jesus is Lord over their lives; they proclaim in word, prayer, and song that the kingdom of God is at hand.

These prayer meetings provide many Christians with an experience of power that they do not find elsewhere. Scripture certainly teaches that there is unlimited power available through the prayer of faith.

> I solemnly assure you, whoever says to this mountain, "Be lifted up and thrown into the sea," and has no inner doubts but believes that what he says will happen, shall have it done for him. I give you my word, if you are ready to believe that you will receive whatever you ask for in prayer, it shall be done for you.
>
> (Mark 11:23-24)

The gifts evidenced in these meetings have their scriptural basis in the context of the prayer meetings of the Church at

Corinth. Paul teaches that these gifts and manifestations are available universally.

> There are different gifts but the same Spirit; there are different ministries but the same Lord; there are different works but the same God who accomplishes all of them in everyone. To each person the manifestation of the Spirit is given for the common good. To one the Spirit gives wisdom in discourse, to another the power to express knowledge. Through the Spirit one receives faith; by the same Spirit another is given the gift of healing, and still another miraculous powers. Prophecy is given to one; to another power to distinguish one spirit from another. One receives the gift of tongues, another that of interpreting the tongues. But it is one and the same Spirit who produces all these gifts, distributing them to each as he wills.
> (1 Cor. 12:4-11. See Rom. 12:4-8)

There is a good basis for viewing these prayer meetings as part of the eucharistic liturgy of the early Church. Today prayer meetings and liturgy are separate events. In modern terminology, prayer meetings would be categorized as para-liturgical celebrations, gatherings which do not take the place of liturgy but support the liturgical life. Such celebrations are designed to be distinct events. For example, the Bible Vigil, the most common para-liturgical celebration of the 1960's, consisted of a special celebration of the Word of God in readings, enthronement of the Bible, homilies, and song. It gave an opportunity for the assembly to concentrate on the Word apart from the eucharistic sacrifice, but also reinforced the place of Scripture and homily in the liturgy. In fact, some of the rubrics of the Bible Vigil have been incorporated as regular optional procedures in the eucharistic liturgy. The prayer meeting is an integral event which need not be attached to the Eucharist, but it *has* developed powerful modes of prayer, and has already provided the eucharistic liturgy with forms of proclamation such as prophecy, forms of praise such as singing in tongues, and forms of petition such as laying on of hands.

Christians can celebrate Church aside from prayer meetings in many ways, but the prayer meeting does best lay the foundation for a vitally alive celebration of the eucharistic liturgy. Christians who commit their lives to one another in community, Christians who serve the poor and perform other apostolic works together are building their Church relationship. However, Christians who do these and *also* pray together and, especially, praise together, are celebrating Church and are best prepared to celebrate the sacraments in power.

But what makes these sacred moments or sacraments unique and essential? Many a Christian who has met Jesus in prayer or especially at a prayer meeting has wondered, why sacraments? If I can know the Jesus who loves me, heals me, teaches me in prayer celebrations, in celebrating Church, why do I need the seven sacraments also? The answer lies in understanding how we encounter Jesus in the sacraments.

4

Encountering Jesus

In the sacraments, Jesus pledges his presence in power. We know absolutely that he will be there and that we will be offered the grace and power we need. The sacraments are Jesus' way of continuing his walk on earth. In them, we meet the same Jesus who walked with the disciples.

The disciples met a Jesus who loved them. If they were sick, he healed their illnesses. If they were bound by evil, he freed them. Where they were ignorant, he taught them. If they were hungry and without food, he fed them. The disciples knew this Jesus who could meet their needs and call them forth in power to meet the needs of others. The disciples knew that Jesus, being informed that a 12-year-old girl was dying, would move to heal her as he healed the daughter of Jairus (Luke 8:49-56). Jesus' life was filled with meeting the special moments of others' needs.

To see Jesus' loving care, consider the experience of one disciple—Peter. Peter knew Jesus in so many loving ways. He knew a Jesus who would provide the sustenance of life in bread and fish, who would remove the danger of a storm, and would supply money for taxes. Peter knew a healing Jesus, especially when Jesus healed his mother-in-law. He knew the correcting and forgiving Jesus. He knew the Jesus who counseled him and who washed his feet. He knew a Jesus who would empower him to shepherd the people.

Now the sacrament rooted in Jesus is designed to make saving grace as freely and visibly present to us as Jesus was present to his followers on the journeys through Galilee. Sacraments only have meaning for us if we understand that they flow directly from the physical presence of Jesus as the Sacrament of God given to man at the Incarnation. We should again remind ourselves that Jesus continues in his body, the Church, and that the whole Church is therefore the Sacrament of Christ.

Sacraments are proclaimed by the Church for special moments in our lives, for significant points in our journey to complete union with God. Baptism with Confirmation is the beginning of our salvation. The Eucharist completes initiation and provides the ongoing sustenance of our spiritual lives. These three sacraments have been celebrated as solemn moments of grace from the earliest days of Christianity, as recorded in the Acts of the Apostles. Even the sacrament of Orders was implied in the setting aside of disciples for special ministry. However, it was more than a thousand years before the Church decided on the word "sacrament" and specifically taught that the sacraments were seven in number. The Church as the Sacrament of Christ proclaimed and exercised the powers of healing, forgiving, reconciling, confirming as witnesses, solemnizing marriages, and calling forth men as deacons, priests, and bishops. But these were not specific as graces of seven sacraments until the eleventh century.

This evolution of the meaning of sacrament through the experience of the Church is the basis for experiencing sacraments not as objective entities but as personal encounters. We celebrate sacraments because, over the centuries, the Church understood sacraments as a vital way for Christians to meet Jesus. Sacraments are best understood as Jesus reaching out to us, now saving, now forgiving, now consecrating and blessing, now uniting, now empowering, and now healing. The sacraments are one in that they flow from Jesus through the Church which is one. They are many in that they are different actions for different times and situations.

Over the years, rituals evolved to symbolize the specific action of grace in each sacrament. Special garments, words, and gestures developed to enrich the experiences and communicate the solemnity of what was happening. But, in time, the people of God became less aware of the origin of these rituals. The Church began to emphasize the automatic effect of the sacraments, called in theology the *ex opere operato* action. It minimized the personal response of the people to the saving action of the Lord, called the *ex opere operantis* action. The personal encounter was more and more overlooked. The solemn ritual in itself was more and more expected to meet all spiritual needs and satisfy responsibility for prayer and worship. Today, in the charismatic renewal, this personal encounter in the sacraments is again being recognized and expected.

But just how do we personally encounter Jesus in the sacraments?

The early Church struggled with the absence of a personal Jesus. The apostles had encountered a Jesus they could touch, embrace, and speak with face-to-face. Their stories of life with Jesus were the substance of the good news in the early Church. The new Christians were told: "Jesus is coming again soon." Paul preached to them to be ready, not to worry about changing their status in life: if married, stay married; if single, stay single. Jesus is coming soon. Maranatha!

Christians waited for the imminent coming; but waiting became more difficult as the years passed. Instead of seeing Jesus, Christians experienced more difficulties. Persecution and famine were upon them. Rival groups appeared in the Church. The Judaizers feuded with the Gentile Christians. People began to say: I belong to Paul, I to Apollos, I to Peter.

These difficulties and rivalries were bound to discourage Christians who longed to encounter Jesus, but who seemed only to encounter more problems. Paul seemingly had told them that they would not see death before Jesus would come. Yet they saw their friends and relatives die.

In this context, Luke narrates the Emmaus event in the twenty-fourth chapter of his gospel. He narrates the story as it was preached—to give new hope to those who were becoming discouraged. The purpose of the preached account was to enable the early Christians to make the transition which the disciples had to make on their Emmaus journey. For us, as contemporary Christians, the Emmaus story provides us with a similar lesson about the way we are to meet Jesus in the sacraments.

Luke describes the two disciples, discouraged because of the absence of Jesus, on their way from Jerusalem to Emmaus. They have left the brethren in Jerusalem; as they walk along, they review the events of the crucifixion of Jesus. Certainly Luke is making reference here to all Christians who might be discouraged by not knowing Jesus now in their lives.

The disciples meet a stranger. They expect little from him, for he doesn't seem to know about Jesus. However, when he starts to speak of the Scriptures, their hearts burn within them and they urge him to stay with them and share the meal. During the meal, the stranger "took the bread, pronounced the blessing, then broke the bread and began to distribute it to them" (Luke 24:30). As soon as he does this, the disciples recognize him. In other words, as soon as the Eucharist is celebrated, those present will recognize Jesus as not being absent from their lives, but as being truly present there.

In Luke's narrative, Jesus disappears the moment the disciples recognize him through the breaking of the bread. To the early Church, Luke is saying that once you see Jesus present in the Eucharist with your eyes of faith, you do not need to

have him appear to you as he appeared to the disciples on the
road to Emmaus.

In Luke's narrative, the encounter changes the disciples.
They become men of hope. They change the direction of their
journey, no longer leaving the body of the brethren. They turn
about and rush back to Jerusalem to proclaim the good news:
Jesus is alive and we have encountered him. Luke's teaching
to the early Church is: meet Jesus in the Eucharist and you
too will know your hearts burning within you through his
word, and your spirits will rejoice with new hope as you share
in his body and blood. You will then desire to be more closely
united to the brethren, and you will change the direction of
your life to live at the heart of the Christian community.

This story is the model for all Eucharistic celebrations. We
are called to meet a Jesus who loves us, feeds us with his
words and with his intimate loving presence. The key to encountering Jesus in the sacraments is to seek that same loving
Jesus who met Peter on so many levels and transformed his
life, the same Jesus who met the disciples on the road to Emmaus. The key to the sacraments is to expect nothing less from
them than what a loving encounter with Jesus on the shores of
the Sea of Galilee would have produced. Indeed, we should
expect more, because the death, resurrection, and glorification
of Jesus has released saving power. This power was poured
out on Pentecost and is given to us all. The sacraments are
special channels by which this saving power comes into our
lives. They are not the only way we encounter Jesus and the
power of his resurrection, for we meet the Lord in his word
and through his Spirit within us. Nevertheless, the sacraments
are special moments set aside for a solemn encounter.

In addition to approaching the sacraments with expectant
faith, we must also understand the concept of covenant if we
are to personally encounter Jesus. Through Jesus, the Sacrament of God, we were invited into the solemn new covenant

with God and to become the new people of God. We do not meet Jesus as individuals. It is not a "Jesus and me" encounter. Rather, each individual—one member of the body of Christ, one person among the People of God—meets Jesus who is in convenanted union with the Father. We cannot meet Jesus without being brought to the Father. Jesus cannot receive us except within the framework of the Church and all of God's people. It is vitally important that we understand this.

A covenant is a contract between persons in which a new relationship of some sort is established. A marriage covenant establishes a marital union and changes a relationship between a man and a woman into that of a husband and wife. A covenant among peoples can make them citizens of the same nation or allies against a common enemy. A covenant can establish relationships so that people become partners in an enterprise or common heirs of an inheritance. A covenant is a special form of a contract but contract embraces agreements about property rights over goods and materials which would not properly fall under covenant. Covenant may include these matters, but primarily orders relationships among persons and usually signifies a new level of friendship or intimacy.

Many forms of covenant prevailed among the ancient peoples. Yahweh used one of these forms of covenant to establish his relationship with Abraham and his descendants. The crux of the covenant consisted in an exchange of promises summarized by the formula: "I will be your God and you will be my people." A sovereign partnership between God and man resulted. This was effected through a covenant form irrevocable in nature. Neither party had the right to renounce or withdraw.

Yahweh graciously chose Israel as his portion, his chosen people. Israel chose Yahweh to be its God to the exclusion of all others. This covenant was a consequence of a series of alliances with Abraham (Genesis 15:9-12, 17 f.), then with all

Israel at Sinai (Exodus 20, 34). After Sinai, Israel repeatedly violated the covenant prescripts. Nevertheless, Yahweh pledged to David a messianic covenant in which David was assured a descendant who would be God's Son and through whom David's house would remain forever (2 Sam. 7). This new covenant was proclaimed by the prophets as a law to be written on the hearts of men in the reign of the messiah.

Jesus is the Messiah of the new covenant. He solemnly pledges his life to do the Father's will. He sheds his own blood in sacrifice to seal the new and eternal covenant between God and his people, the Church. He institutes the Eucharist as the solemn renewal and celebration of the covenant. The pledge of the new covenant is the Holy Spirit poured out in the hearts of God's people. In the power of the Holy Spirit, people can now proclaim externally the reality within. They can say: "Jesus is Lord;" they can call God "Our Father."

Jesus is present in the sacraments within the covenant context. The depth of the encounter with Jesus depends on how deeply we enter the covenant. The more completely we give ourselves to live as God's people under the lordship of Jesus, the more meaningful is the encounter. Likewise the more completely we come as God's people rather than as individuals, the more totally we can celebrate who we are and be present to the Lord. Thus, the more a people is together as Christian community, the more fully can they celebrate the sacraments.

The covenant celebrations vary in fruitfulness depending on the depth of the individual commitment to God, the clarity of the identification with the Church as God's people, and the degree of unity of the local community as part of the covenanted people. In practical terms, this means that the power of the encounter with Jesus will increase as the individual Christian deepens in faith and dedication, expresses his role as a member of the Church, and shares his life with fellow

Christians. This is evident to those who have experienced a eucharistic liturgy where those present have deep personal commitments to the Lord and to one another. This experience is striking compared to another liturgy where those present were strangers to each other or had made a superficial commitment to the Lord.

We should note some conclusions from these truths. A covenant commitment is necessarily part of the nature of celebrating a sacrament. This commitment is first to the Lord and then to the people of God. This is not just an internal commitment, but is to have some visible expression. This commitment should first be shown in our relationships with those most proximate to us, those with whom we are called to share our lives. Others should be able to see in the pattern of our living that we are committed in a sacred way to others. The commitment should also be evidenced in our commitment to those beyond our immediate community. In the love of Jesus, we are in some way bound to all the people of God, to all who are called to be among the people of God. In other words, in every sacrament we celebrate our commitment to support all our brothers and sisters in the Lord. This commitment takes on a lived expression in feeding the hungry, clothing the naked, caring for orphans and widows, freeing those under oppression and in bringing about justice and service to the poor. This social dimension is present in each sacrament, though admittedly its expression varies depending on the circumstances.

Thus, as we consider each sacrament, we should look not just to the Jesus whom we encounter but to all the people related to Jesus and covenanted to us. We are saved and healed, strengthened and fed as a member of *this covenanted people*. We cannot escape this truth, though we can approach the sacraments with varying levels of awareness of its relevance.

Each sacrament has its special role with regard to covenant; in each sacramental celebration we are called to a new place or a new deepening of our place with God's covenanted people. Jesus commissioned Baptism as the way into this new covenant. As the Church developed under the guidance of the Holy Spirit, Confirmation was formalized as the completion of this initiation whereby Christians were to know their baptism with "spirit and fire." With Confirmation, Christians were not only to be incorporated into the people of God but were to witness to the new covenant. In the Eucharist, Christians celebrate the new covenant and open their lives to the Spirit, deepening the covenant relationship in their lives. In Penance, Christians are reconciled to the people of God; they repent of infidelity to the covenant, and the binding relationship is restored and deepened. In Matrimony and Orders, special covenant relationships are established both to function within the people of God and to symbolize the broader covenant with God. Finally, the nature of covenant as a healing, reconciling, life-giving relationship is celebrated through the power of the Anointing of the Sick.

While it is important to understand the sacraments rightly as covenant celebrations, it is equally important to approach them with expectant faith. We should expect to encounter Jesus in power, here and now, and expect the sacraments to deepen our covenant relationship with God and man. This lively, expectant faith means to reach out to touch the hem of the garment of Jesus, saying, if only I do, I will be healed. It means that the ministers expect power will go forth from them. It means that the community members call forth this faith from one another. The more the words and actions in the sacraments on the part of both priest and people truly represent Jesus present in power, and the living covenant relationship to be experienced, the more expectant faith will grow among us.

The most important point is that we know who we are, what

we need, and what we expect of the Lord in each sacrament. We are to be ready to meet him, fully alive to his presence. Each sacrament is different, just as, for example, an encounter with a brother or sister in a hospital, at a wedding reception, or in a prison would be different in our lives.

But we never meet Jesus alone. We always meet him as Church, as a people celebrating that they are Church. We renew and deepen our covenant with one another and the Lord in each meeting.

With this foundation established for celebrating sacraments, we now propose a working definition, based on that foundation, to aid in understanding our treatment of individual sacraments.

A sacrament is a visible sign of God's desire and pledge to deepen his relationship with us. It promises the gift of grace we seek: healing, nourishing, cleansing, freeing, consecrating, blessing, empowering us to accept his reign in our lives and deepen our covenant with him and his people.

This definition is useful for understanding how the Church develops in the fullness of its life and how it expresses itself in the seven particular sacraments.

In the following chapters we will attempt to show:

-the problems which currently affect the reception and celebration of individual sacraments;

-how the Church, as it deepens in its covenant with God, can grow in its power to signify and communicate the saving presence of Jesus;

-how the Church truly alive can encounter Jesus in the solemn moments of its life—the sacraments;

-how these solemn moments or sacraments have their own

symbols and particular graces to signify the presence of the Lord;

-finally, how pastoral practice needs to be adapted to meet these vital truths.

5

Penance

We treat Penance first because the analysis of the problems in this sacrament will provide an implicit basis for treating the other sacraments. In many ways Penance has been *the* problem sacrament. Because of the complex pastoral problems, it was the final sacrament to be revised under the directives of the Vatican Council.* It is the sacrament most liable to fall into disuse according to present trends. And yet, we and others associated with us have found new power and new life in this sacrament. Thus, we feel that Penance presents the clearest contrast between current practice and foreseeable improvements.

To think of Penance is to stir up challenging questions. What is the future of the sacrament of Penance? Will it continue to fall into greater disuse? Will the sacrament continue to have less and less importance in the lives of Catholics? What will be the effect of the New Rite of Penance?

Most Catholics of the older generation grew up with fixed ideas about heaven, hell, and purgatory. They knew sin was the key to their future. If a person died in mortal sin, he went to hell. If he died in venial sin or without atoning for the temporal effects of sin already forgiven, he went to purgatory and then to heaven. If he was particularly holy and died

*"Constitution on the Sacred Liturgy," par. 72.

neither in sin nor with temporal punishment due to sin, he could go directly to heaven. It was very clear how important sin was in determining a person's future.

There was little problem determining what was sin. Sin was what violated the law of God. The law was listed in the commandments of God and the commandments of the Church. Sins against these commandments were described in detail in catechisms and in booklets which were used to prepare for confession. Sins were categorized into mortal and venial on the basis of seriousness of the nature of the violation. This was called gravity of matter. A person committed a mortal sin if the sin was grave in nature, and if the person did it with sufficient reflection on what he or she was doing and with full consent of the will. Whenever a person committed a mortal sin he would go to hell if he died immediately. We were taught that God in his goodness was not trying to trap us and that he would give good men time to repent. But it was not possible to rely on that. Once someone committed a mortal sin, he was to attempt a perfect act of contrition. If he succeeded in repenting with perfect sorrow, the sin was forgiven. But if he failed, he had to confess the sin to a priest as soon as possible. In confession, he would receive the added grace so that the sin confessed with imperfect sorrow would be forgiven. The grace of the sacrament provided what was lacking in the contrition outside the sacrament.

Thus, the way the sacrament of Penance worked was clear and overwhelmingly important. People knew the rules and adopted patterns of using the sacrament. Those who concluded they had committed a mortal sin immediately knew they had to arrange for confession. Those habitually only in venial sin adopted a pattern such as weekly or monthly confession. They wanted these sins taken care of and they wanted the added graces that would both take away the temporal punishment of sin and help them to avoid sin. Others would go to confession before communion, and some would put it off until Christmas or Easter. Every Catholic was aware that he or she must go to communion once during the Easter season and that this normally meant confession before the day of communion.

The rules and procedures were clear. The only matters in question were the penance that the priest would assign and the comments he would make. However, these were highly important matters, since there could be a great difference between a few Our Fathers and Hail Marys for a penance and more rigorous prayers and acts of reparation. Similarly, some priests would loudly chastise penitents while others would speak only of God's love and mercy. Thus it was important to go to the right priest.

On the whole, Catholics had a clear concept of heaven, hell, purgatory, mortal sin, venial sin, holiness, confession, and penance for sin. They had set ideas which enabled them to organize these areas in a manageable way. In a way, this was extraordinary, because these concepts involved mysteries beyond man's understanding. Certainly no one can understand heaven or hell. The nature of God, sin against him, and forgiveness by him are also beyond comprehension. Therefore, the principles around which Catholics organized these realities were most important. They enabled people to deal with truths which transcended their comprehension. The theological term for such organizing principles is "myth." We are all familiar with fictional myths such as fairy tales. *But myth in theological terminology has a very different definition: It is a means by which realities are organized so that we can deal with them.*

While it would be better for theological purposes to use the term "myth," because of the common tendency to associate this word only with fiction or untruth, we will employ the equivalent terminology of "organizing principle" or framework for the remainder of this section.

At the time of the Second Vatican Council, the pattern of confession which organized the truths of sin and eternal reward began to be less helpful. This organizing principle did not provide answers for new questions. There was a growing concern that confession was not as effective as it should be in enabling people to avoid sin and live more holy lives. Penitents seemed to be repeating the same sins, receiving the same penances and admonitions. They grew to expect that neither their list of sins, their penances, nor the admonitions would change. At best, the sacrament seemed to be a holding action. The priest was frustrated because he could do little to enable the penitent to overcome the habitual sins. So the priest frequently geared his words to help the penitent overcome discouragement.

The second area not handled by the organizing principle of Penance was sexuality. Beginning in 1965, the prevalent teachings in the Church on sexual morality challenged the idea that all sins against the sixth and ninth commandments were mortal. These teachings questioned whether some matters were really grave, and also maintained that full consent of the will was frequently absent in sins of passion. People began to revise their confession of sexual sins. They resorted to general statements such as "failing against purity" and "not living in the right way." They withheld some areas from confession on the basis that they no longer believed them sinful. Penitents started to reject the lists for examination of conscience, saying that the categorized sins did not meet the realities of their lives. Some maintained that sins of omission in failing to love in the family were usually more important than an isolated act of passion. Loving and failing to love emerged more and more as the standards of morality accepted by young people.

A third area not handled by the confession framework involved social justice issues. The country was in the midst of a civil rights movement, soon to be followed by anti-poverty and peace campaigns. Finally, a comprehensive liberation theology emerged which put top priority on freeing all minorities from oppression of any sort. The confession framework was not able to give answers to the new questions about sins against social justice. More and more people considered personal, private sins as less important than cooperating in the sins of society against the blacks, the poor, the Mexican Americans, and the Puerto Ricans. Television made the Vietnam War real and personal. Many persons accepted as personally sinful those actions which supported the war. Others thought actions which undermined American's military effort were sins.

A fourth area of questioning emerged from the work of new theologians. Father Charles Curran was the best-known member of a school of moral theologians who taught that mortal sin required much more of the sinner than was formerly believed. They spoke of the fundamental option by which a person chose for or against God. They taught that people elected this fundamental choice through a series of individual actions and that, ordinarily, such a series was necessary before anyone could commit a mortal sin. Other concepts were altered. The perfect contrition necessary for repentance only meant heartfelt sorrow; it was increasingly viewed as something within the ordinary person's ability to do. Purgatory was understood not so much as a place of suffering but rather as a place of purification for heaven—an anteroom of the heavenly dwelling. A new trend in preaching emphasized the good news and the fact that the kingdom of God was here. The kingdom has already come—though it would still come more fully in the future. People began to doubt if there were any persons at all who went to hell. It began to look like one had to be an exceptionally evil person to go to hell.

Finally, new teachings in pastoral practice developed. No longer did sermons emphasize the weekly or monthly confession. No longer could one be sure what the confessor would consider serious or sinful at all. And then the encyclical *Humanae Vitae* created the sensational issue, as the Pope taught that artificial birth control was sinful. A group of respected moral theologians taught that the Pope had not maintained this teaching as a matter of faith, that is, infallibly. Rather they stated that the teaching could be opposed, and they opposed it. In the confessional, priests began struggling with penitents to determine whether birth control practices were sinful in particular cases. Then new practices developed in granting annulments and allowing the remarried under certain conditions to go to the sacraments.

There were other questions which the confession framework could not handle, but these challenges were already too much—the organizing principle of confession collapsed. With the collapse, Catholics no longer had a clear teaching to organize their understanding of heaven, hell, purgatory, sin, and forgiveness. Without this framework of teaching, confession lost much meaning and people treated it with much less importance. Many ceased to go to the sacrament.

This was not the first time that a useful understanding of the sacrament of Penance had collapsed. In the first centuries, Penance was considered a sacrament for those who had committed public sins of apostasy, murder, and adultery. The bishop assigned rigorous public penances such as fasting, wearing sackcloth, and begging for a year or more, at the end of which absolution could be given. Later, Penance was considered a sacrament to be received only once and then by those who sinned seriously after conversion and baptism. Tertullian taught that the sacrament of Penance, administered in this light, was the second plank of salvation. (Baptism of course, was the first.) To continue the analogy, according to Tertullian, when a person's salvation ship was wrecked through sin, the Church, by the sacrament of Penance, threw him a plank by which that person could be saved.

In the Middle Ages, the tariff concept of Penance developed. Personll, private confession had become the normal practice, but the Church emphasized the penitent's responsibility to make reparation for all sins committed. Heavy penances were assigned, such as a pilgrimage to Jerusalem or bread and water fasts. These burdens were so heavy that various practices developed to lighten them. These practices included having another person satisfy the penance and the granting of indulgences which satisfied the outstanding penances. When these practices became widespread, the tariff concept, like the second plank concept, ceased to be workable.

After the Council of Trent, the Church developed the confessional aspect of the sacrament of Penance. What was being confessed became most important. The new understanding emphasized the correct stating of the sins and the correct judging by the confessor. Penances became lighter; they usually consisted of saying prayers and making retribution for damages caused to another. During these years, the organizing framework of confession which lasted until the 1960's developed. Now this framework no longer provides a sufficient understanding of the sacrament. Many Catholics cannot find peace in either regularly going to confession or in staying away from confession. They have difficulty talking about the sacrament and are not able to evaluate or support most proposed changes in confessional practice.

What will replace the confessional framework of Penance? The teaching of Vatican II and the instructions accompanying the New Rite of Penance put the focus on reconciliation. The rite itself is called a Rite of Reconciliation. The fundamental thrust of the sacrament is to reconcile the penitent with God and his fellow man.

While the new rite of Penance is designed to foster reconciliation, few Catholics are ready for it. Most lack the experience of knowing when they are alienated and when they are reconciled. They hear that under the new rite there are three alternative ways to celebrate the sacrament: (1) Rite for Reconciliation of Individual Penitents; (2) Rite for Reconciliation of Several Penitents with Individual Confession and Absolution; and (3) Rite for Reconciliation of Several Penitents with General Confession and Absolution. Even when these alternative rites are explained, most people respond weakly. They do not see how these new rites will meet their life situations. They are not aware of relationships that have broken down so that reconciliation is necessary. They know that their current spiritual conditioniis not what it should be, but they do not see how the sacrament of Penance can make a difference.

The basic problem is one of relationships. If the person has not had a personal ongoing relationship with the Lord, there is nothing to reconcile. Only someone who has known a personal friendship with the Lord can realize the need to restore that friendship when it has been broken or damaged by sin. Such a person will know that the Holy Spirit is the power which creates the relationship and restores it after sin.

Similarly, if a person has no sense of being part of a Christian community, he will lack appreciation of how his sin damages the life of that community. He will also fail to recognize his need to be forgiven by the community in order to restore his relationship within the community. Such a person needs to understand that he lives under the New Covenant in which God's people are to be a community, the body of Christ. He needs to discover a local community which will give him meaningful relationships with brothers and sisters. Once he discovers his place in the community, he can accept his responsibility to grow in holiness in order to strengthen all the relationships in the community.

When these relationships with the Lord and with members

of his body are established, we can begin talking about how reconciliation through the sacrament is to take place. Specifically, what will penitents need in the sacrament to experience reconciliation? People need to experience a power in the sacrament which touches the deepest areas of alienation in their lives. People need to encounter a forgiving, reconciling Jesus who leads them to identify and repent for their sins, who lets them know they are forgiven, and who shows them the power to change their lives. People need to know experientially that they are reconciled with God and with their brothers and sisters. They need to know new life and new hope.

The experience of Christian communities growing out of the charismatic renewal is teaching us the importance of asking and giving forgiveness. The sins and failings of members of a community frequently are of such a nature that unless there is explicit forgiveness, full reconciliation will never take place. A brother or sister who ignores, ridicules, or deceives another brother or sister needs to repent and to ask forgiveness directly from the injured person. When this forgiveness is given, not only is reconciliation completed but the community is usually stronger for the experience than it was before the injury occurred. This asking and receiving of forgiveness should extend even to areas of doubtful sinfulness. While such mutual forgiveness and reconciliation are not strictly part of the sacrament of Penance, they are necessarily related to it. If such a step has not preceded the sacrament, then a resolution to effect it should be made within the sacrament.

All of the above might sound too idealistic. It is strongly stated because it has been proven to be possible. Since the publication of my book *The Power in Penance* in 1972, I (Fr. M.) have seen these effects continue in the lives of penitents who come seeking them in the sacrament. I have heard testimonies from countless priests about the new power in confession. I have the written statements of 131 priests who attended the National Conference for Priests on Charismatic Renewal at Steubenville in 1975, testifying that they have witnessed new and deeper life coming to their penitents. They testify to healings from resentments, bitterness, migraine headaches, depressions, unhealthy guilt, feelings of hatred, chronic masturbation, and compulsive homosexual actions. These healings have come about because priest and penitent sought out the root of sinfulness in the penitent's life and then prayed that the love of the Lord in the power of the Spirit would heal it. The same priests further report that prophetic words of knowledge, passages of Scripture, directions of wisdom, and other revelatory gifts served as powerful aids in enabling the confessor to help the penitent.

Many such personal testimonies and a discussion of optional models for confession are found in *The Power in Penance*. Here I shall comment on key areas in the new rite of Penance in order to state what is most important to be done in this sacrament.

The rite of individual reconciliation is divided into (1) Reception, (2) Reading the Word, (3) Confession, (4) Prayer of Penitent, (5) Absolution, (6) Proclamation of Praise and Dismissal.

1. In the reception, the priest should establish unity with the penitent so that they will seek together the reconciling Lord to know his will for this time. An example of an appropriate expression is, "May we seek the Lord Jesus together, for he came to call sinners not the just; let us have confidence in him." At the same time, the greeting should be personal enough to put the penitent at ease.

2. In reading the Word of God, the priest might first ask the penitent how he is feeling and then choose an appropriate text. Thus, if the penitent feels cold and indifferent, the priest might read Ezekiel 11:19-20: "I will give them a new heart and put a new spirit within them. I will remove the stony heart

from their bodies, and replace it with a natural heart, so that they will live according to my statutes, and observe and carry out my ordinances; thus they shall be my people and I will be their God."

If the penitent feels discouraged and burdened by his sins, the priest might read Isaiah 53:4: "It was our infirmities that he bore, our sufferings that he endured." Or Romans 8:1: "There is no condemnation now for those who are in Christ Jesus."

If the penitent is caught up in rivalry, resentment, or in nursing the hurts caused by others, the priest might read Matthew 6:14-15: If you forgive the faults of others, your heavenly Father will forgive you yours. If you do not forgive others, neither will your Father forgive you."

Frequently, the penitent will know the appropriate Scripture to be read. Where time permits, prayer and reflection on the Scripture can be beneficial.

3. The confession is meant to be a dialogue in which priest and penitent uncover the principal areas needing reconciliation. They should attempt to find the root of the sinfulness and agree on just what is to be handled in the sacrament. Normally, the priest should discourage the penitent from addressing many areas of sin at one time. At one given time, the penitent can normally only repent from the heart in two or three areas of his life. The priest should seek the guidance of the Spirit as to which areas being mentioned are most important. By carefully listening to the penitent, the priest can detect what area is the main cause of alienation and discern what areas are the basis of the penitent's sorrow and true repentance. These areas should be dealt with; other areas should be put aside as long as they do not involve serious sin. In order to make this decision, the priest will also have to be listening to the Holy Spirit. The Holy Spirit will confirm in the priest's spirit many of the thoughts he has about how to proceed. As he

seeks to know how the Lord would have him help the penitent, the priest will sense freedom, love, or peace in a powerful way.

The priest should be alert to suggesting to the penitent what might be the root cause of the sin. This is most evident in cases where the penitent confesses frequent uncharitableness toward one person. Usually there is an ongoing resentment toward that person based on some past incident that was never properly resolved. The earlier incident where the penitent was offended should be reopened and handled. The penitent needs to forgive the person from the heart and usually go to the person and talk out the problem. Each party should ask forgiveness where warranted. Other times, the uncharitableness may be based on ongoing rivalry. The penitent may be threatened in some way by success the other person is having such as receiving promotions or achieving social popularity. The penitent needs to see this, repent of this possessiveness, and renounce all rivalry.

These roots of confessed sins are present in nearly all areas. A person's resentment against his father who rejected him can cause hatred against God as father, or, such resentment can be the root source of a homosexual problem. Seeing oneself as a hopeless failure can be the root of many sins of escape such as drug addiction, drunkenness, sexual immorality, and envy. Most penitents know the root of their problem. They need to be encouraged to state it. Without such encouragement, the penitent stays with the usual formula for confessing sins and avoids the more personal and revealing area.

Within a few minutes, priest and penitent can usually agree on the areas to be handled. The priest should then propose that after the absolution they pray together for what is most needed: a healing of a wound from a past experience of unlove, a strengthening in resolve and courage, an increase in wisdom or love, or a prayer of authority against forces of evil which are interfering in the penitent's life.

4. The penitent then expresses sorrow for his sins. Ten recommended prayers of sorrow are listed in the Revised Rite However, the priest should encourage the penitent to pray in his own words, because these are usually more effective and sincere expressions of the desires of his heart.

5. In giving absolution, the priest is directed to extend both hands or at least one hand over the penitent. This is the traditional sign of absolution. It also leads naturally to prayers for healing and strengthening.

6. Finally, the priest says, "Give thanks to the Lord for he is good," and the penitent responds, "His mercy endures forever." The priest dismisses the penitent saying, "The Lord has freed you from your sins. Go in peace," or similar words.

The second rite is the Rite for Reconciliation of Several Penitents with Individual Confession and Absolution. This rite is based on the communal penance services which have been utilized for a number of years. The rite gives a formal structure for such a service. There is a greeting, opening prayer, celebration of the Word of God through reading and homily, and then a rite of reconciliation which involves a minister leading in general formulas of confession of sin and the people answering with, "We pray you, hear us," or a similar response. The people then go to a private place for individual confession of sins and individual absolution. After this, they return to the assembly for the proclamation of praise.

This rite has many possibilities, especially for those who are used to prayer meetings. There are opportunities for song and praise that parallel the prayer meeting. The homily is an opportunity to utilize an insight gained by those of us in the inner healing ministry. This is that people repent and seek out the sacrament of Penance not so much because they become aware of what they did wrong, but rather because they become more aware of God's love for them, especially when they have been unfaithful. A homily directed to the love of the Lord to heal, make whole, bring new life into dead relationships, restore families, and free those bound by habits of sin can proclaim the truth that frees and can lead people to repentance and the sacrament.

This type of homily stands in contrast to the traditional practices of preachers who were inclined to preach about the evil of sin in order to foster repentance. What we have learned is that emphasizing sin has a discouraging and oppressive effect on people. They tend to withdraw, feel the situation is hopeless, and seek escape. Preaching about God's love for them is often highly effective. If people experience God's desire for a personal relationship with them, they will seek to put everything right so that they can live as fully as possible in that relationship. When people come to a new realization that they are loved by God, then they want to respond with a new conversion to God. Similarly, when people realize they are loved by brothers and sisters, they want to respond to that love by eliminating the barriers to a loving relationship. Therefore, homilies directed to the personal love of the Lord for his people and the supportive love of the community can easily lead into the need for people to live these relationships. Such homilies are most effective in fostering repentance, conversion, and reconciliation. People want to love and be loved; they need to know it is possible to live those relationships here and now.

The third rite of Penance is referred to as general absolution and is called "The Rite for Reconciliation of Several Penitents with General Confession and Absolution." The name of the rite does not include the word "individual" since the confession is done in general terms in a group of people with everyone receiving absolution at the same time. As in the second rite, the priest proceeds through the homily. Then he announces, "Will those of you who wish to receive sacramental absolution please kneel and acknowledge that you are sinners." There follows a prayer of confession and the priest administers absolution.

This third rite is not an ordinary means of receiving the sacrament. Its use is restricted to cases of danger of death and grave needs as determined by the bishop of the diocese. The Church requires that those who receive absolution under this rite confess their serious sins again at a later time for individual absolution. This requirement is a clear teaching that reconciliation means more than having sins absolved. When a person comes for individual absolution, he is opening his life to discernment, instruction, and healing prayer in a way that is not possible under general absolution. We do not seek forgiveness from our friends by making general statements in a crowd. Neither can we know full reconciliation by confessing our sin in a large group. We will be forgiven, but the restoration of the relationship with God and our brothers and sisters requires a more personal encounter.

The second and third rites of Penance, since they deal with penitents as a group or community, have particular value in emphasizing the social dimension of sin and the need to restore community relationships. They tend to counteract the "God-and-me-alone" syndrome that grew up under the confession framework. They emphasize instead the teaching of Paul to the Colossians:

> Because you are God's chosen ones, holy and beloved, clothe yourselves with heartfelt mercy, with kindness, humility, meekness and patience. Bear with one another; forgive whatever grievances you have against one another. Forgive as the Lord has forgiven you. Over all these virtues put on love, which binds the rest together

and makes them perfect. Christ's peace must reign in your hearts, since as members of the one body you have been called to that peace.

(Col. 3:12-15)

(Sr. A.) Many persons have testified to new life and to the healing of relationships through the sacrament of Reconciliation and can witness by their lives to the truth of what has been written thus far in this chapter.

But how does a person prepare for such an encounter with his God?

First, I believe it is important to remember that most healing in the sacrament *flows from* an attitude of repentance and a desire for conversion. However, it is equally important to remember, as we stated on page 53: "People repent and seek out the sacrament of Penance not so much because they become aware of what they did wrong, but rather, because they become more aware of God's love for them, especially when they have been unfaithful."

About four years ago, that truth became a personal reality for me. I had been baptized in the Spirit for over a year and that encounter with God had been gradually touching many areas of my life. However, until this particular occasion, the sacrament of Reconciliation was still a routine venture. On this occasion, I followed my usual pattern of confession: I examined my conscience, mentally listed where I had failed, made an act of contrition, and then went to a priest to recite my sins and receive absolution. So I thought!

After reciting my "laundry list" (as I've since come to refer to it), the priest asked me if there was anything else. I promptly said "no." He responded: "Are you sorry for *anything* you've mentioned?" I was a bit surprised and self-righteously said, "Yes, of course, *everything*." Then there was a pause, and in that moment I realized with a clarity I had never seen before that I wasn't experiencing any genuine contrition. I had participated in a mechanical ritual that satisfied an obligation and made me "feel good." I was sorry for my sins in an abstract intellectual way, but my personal relationship with the Lord had not yet reached a level where a desire to repent and *be converted* could genuinely spring from my heart.

As I grappled with this realization I discovered that the priest hearing my confession had been praying for me. I saw in that prayer a sign of someone who desired my greatest good. It gave me courage to say, "I don't think I'm genuinely sorry for anything I've said"—that is, sorry to the point that I would be willing to allow God's healing grace to touch an area and *expect* a particular pattern of acting to change. (Up to that point I had been satisfied with reciting sins followed by absolution. This was a pattern which could be repeated weekly or monthly with the same sins for years.)

Now, realizing how much more God had for me, I began to *understand* what it could mean to be transformed and healed through the sacrament. The priest and I prayed silently for a moment. Then he said that while he could give me absolution if I requested it, since "all conditions were fulfilled," he would prefer to wait until I had experienced a real desire for and openness to conversion. I was stunned—no one had ever hesitated to grant me absolution. Yet I understood. We prayed together again that I could receive what God desired me to know.

For four months I allowed the truth of God's love to penetrate a hardness of heart I hadn't even known existed. (My reflections on this experience can be found on pages 23-25.) As this began to happen, I also began to desire that my life be in right order. I began to realize that I did not have to continue in habitual patterns of sin if I were willing to be open to have them change. I began to know his love for me at such a depth that I could see his great joy when I sought his forgiveness. "Lord, have mercy," became a *personal* prayer.

The sacrament of Reconciliation had come alive!

The father of the Prodigal Son runs out to meet us with open arms *every time* we desire to come home. We need to know that! We need to know that no matter how great our sins, the Father only asks that we turn to him and seek his mercy. If we do, we then *experience* the truth of the words, "as far as the east is from the west, so far has he put our transgressions from us" (Ps. 103:12).

There is, however, a great pitfall with the small but daily sins and failings of our lives. We can begin to so take them for granted that we fail to see how they block a growing relationship with the Lord. We excuse such sins with, "That's human nature." It is true that we are sinners. We are not perfect. We will always need forgiveness. However, the more we can see the patterns of our daily lives in the light of God's *personal* love for each of us, the more we will want to respond in a repentant way to that love in even the smallest areas of our daily lives.

As we see for ourselves the transformation God so desires, we will freely allow him more and more to exercise his lordship over us, a lordship over our sins, our pain and our weakness through the sacrament that leads not only to healing and wholeness for ourselves, but for all those who are part of our lives.

Ultimately, then, the sacrament of Reconciliation should be seen in the broader context of the mission of Jesus to reconcile the world to the Father.

As Paul writes to the Corinthians:

> . . . if anyone is in Christ, he is a new creation. The old order has passed away; now all is new! All this has been done by God, who has reconciled us to himself through

Christ and has given us the ministry of reconciliation. I mean that God, in Christ, was reconciling the world to himself, not counting men's transgressions against them, and that he has entrusted the message of reconciliation to us. This makes us ambassadors for Christ, God as it were appealing through us. We implore you in Christ's name: be reconciled to God. For our sakes God made him who did not know sin, to be sin, so that in him we might become the very holiness of God.

(2 Cor. 5:17-21)

.

The next three chapters discuss the sacraments of initiation: Baptism, Confirmation, and the Eucharist. These were administered as part of one sacramental action in the early Church. There is ample evidence that Confirmation is a renewal and extension of Baptism and that both find their completion only in the Eucharist. As sound as this may be theologically, it does not meet the current pastoral situation. The current practice of infant Baptism is followed some years later by Penance and the Eucharist and again a few years later by Confirmation. We will treat the sacraments in light of this pastoral situation yet in their proper order as sacraments of initiation.

6

Baptism

A certain Pharisee named Nicodemus, a member of the Jewish Sanhedrin, came to him at night. "Rabbi," he said, "we know you are a teacher come from God, for no man can perform signs and wonders such as you perform unless God is with him." Jesus gave him this answer:

> "I solemnly assure you,
> no one can see the reign of God
> unless he is begotten from above."

"How can a man be born again once he is old?" retorted Nicodemus. "Can he return to his mother's womb and be born over again?" Jesus replied:

> "I solemnly assure you,
> no one can enter into God's kingdom
> without being begotten of water and Spirit.
> Flesh begets flesh,
> Spirit begets Spirit.
> Do not be surprised that I tell you
> you must be begotten from above. . . ."

(John 3:1-7)

These striking statements from John's Gospel lay the foundation for a true understanding of Baptism. Although all Christians today believe in this sacrament, it is possible that many might be shocked as Nicodemus to hear what being born again really means.

Too often in the past the sacrament of Baptism has been lost midst a scurry in the back of the church. Even today many people gather around a baptismal font while babies are crying, godparents are struggling to be of help: unbuttoning the dress, getting the pacifier. Everyone is trying to remember their lines. Parents and relatives are usually preoccupied with how the baby is acting: smiling, crying, sleeping. The priest is frequently trying to be heard over the noise and confusion. He has a sense of a three-ring circus with each group of people interested only in the reactions of the baby they came to see. There is a temptation to shout, "Who knows what is really happening?"

While the revised rite of Baptism has stressed the meaning of the sacrament and some parishes have been successful in incorporating the baptismal rite with the Eucharistic liturgy, most people still see Baptism as something the priest does to the child to get him into the Church. Most people who are present still believe they are onlookers, in no way important to the sacrament. Most people still regard their own Baptism simply as the first of a series of sacraments.

Do we realize that in Baptism Jesus is encountered as Savior? Do we truly know that in this sacrament Jesus saves the one baptized from a kingdom of darkness and evil and brings the newly baptized into a kingdom of light and eternal life? Do we know that through the saving power of Christ's death and resurrection, the life-giving water of the Holy Spirit is poured out on the newly baptized as a free gift and enables the child of the flesh to live as the adopted daughter or son of God? Through Baptism, the child, born of the love of two people, is now born of water and spirit into the kingdom of light.

The newly baptized person actually steps from one kingdom to another. He chooses, through the power of Jesus Christ in his Spirit, the freedom of the sons and daughters of God. He chooses to be unbound and set free from the powers of darkness—to enter the kingdom of God. By his own choice, or implicitly through his parents' faith, the newly baptized person desires to put his life under the lordship of Jesus—under his reign—and the character of Baptism signs and seals him forever.

The parish or Christian community needs to realize the vital importance of assuring a totally dependent and vulnerable infant the full protection of God's kingdom in its life by presenting the child, *as a community,* for the immersion unto life that is Baptism. The community needs to recognize that through Baptism it is receiving a new member into its midst. It must be willing—as parents, godparents, relatives or members of the Christian community—to firmly commit itself to support the growth of one who is newly signed and sealed in the name of Jesus for the kingdom of our Father.

In the rite itself, it is important that the whole community be gathered together for this event. As much as possible, the baptismal ceremony should be marked by communal participation. Singing, processions, vocal responses by all, and pauses for communal prayer can emphasize such participation. During the times of prayer, the members of the community might extend hands toward the infant. They should pray in two ways: a prayer of authority rebuking all evil, and a prayer of petition for all graces to come upon the baptized. Each Christian should use this time to renew his own baptismal commitment and to deepen his covenant relationship with all his brothers and sisters. The community should hold sacred the moment of Baptism when Jesus is present as Savior.

The community should be aware of the meaning of the elements of Baptism. The water means a cleansing into new life; the lighted candle is the sign of the kingdom of light into which the baptized is entering; the white garment is the wedding garment of the saints; the sign of the cross signifies that the Trinity now dwells in the baptized.

The minister should directly proclaim at this moment that this *is* a time of spiritual victory. The powers of the Church are overcoming the forces of evil. In the case of infants, the parents request Baptism for the child, give it a name, and make a solemn commitment to accept responsibility to train the child in the faith and to form him in obedience to the commandments of God. The godparents agree to help in these tasks. Then, in the presence of the Christian community, the celebrant welcomes those to be baptized, and traces the sign of the cross on the foreheads. This is a prayer of authority in which the celebrant claims the infant for Jesus as Savior. It should be proclaimed as such.

The liturgy of the word follows, and while various options are possible in the choice of readings, all of them indicate a personal encounter with Jesus. They proclaim the truth of what is happening in the sacrament. It is important that the person who reads the Scripture be able to convey that understanding so that the congregation may truly hear and respond.

The prayers of the faithful should offer time for the assembled members of the community to pray from their hearts for the child and for the grace to accept their responsibility in receiving this new life.

The prayer of exorcism follows. Here the priest can choose between two prayers. The first prayer proclaims victory over Satan and the kingdom of darkness and prays that the child be free from original sin and become a temple of glory. The second prayer makes no mention of Satan or original sin, but it speaks of fighting the devil and freeing the child from the slavery of sin and the power of darkness. Whichever prayer is used, the congregation should realize that Jesus' victory over the kingdom of evil is real and absolutely needed in the lives of all who are to pass from the bondage of slavery to the freedom of the children of God.

The reality of spiritual warfare should remain in focus as the rite proceeds. As oil is used to strengthen the child, hands are laid on him in silence, and the baptismal water is empowered through a blessing, the celebrant should proclaim a clear rejection of Satan and all his works and promises. The parents and godparents are called to respond by professing their faith in each person of the Trinity.

Immersion is the preferred form of Baptism; it best portrays the sign of emerging into new life through the total cleansing of water. In one parish we are familiar with, the pastor with the parents raise the child from the water and lift him for all the congregation to see. Such symbolic action reflects the victory of Baptism. Other signs of victory at this moment include the congregation's response, the white garment which the child receives, and the lighted candle.

The final prayer over ears and mouth, while optional, is significant. Touching the ears and mouth of the newly baptized the celebrant prays: "The Lord Jesus made the deaf hear and the dumb speak. May he soon touch your ears to receive his word and your mouth to proclaim his faith, to the praise and glory of God the Father."

In November 1972, I (Fr. M.) baptized my niece. In May 1973, I learned she was deaf. Her parents informed me that they had consulted many experts but that none gave them hope. She was diagnosed as totally deaf. As I listened to the story, I felt a movement of faith within me. I went to my niece's room and prayed for her for about 20 minutes. I placed my fingers in her ears and anointed her with oil. I left, assured in my spirit that something had happened. Two weeks later, my brother slammed the door of her room and she cried. He took her to the doctor who found her hearing exceptionally good, better than normal. Recently, I learned through my brother that the doctor attributes the change directly to the hand of God.

I believe that I was still acting as the baptismal minister in that healing even as I anointed her with oil. I am also determined in the future to pray within the baptismal rite for the Lord to heal whatever is defective in the child.

During the rite, there is also an appropriate time to pray over the child for inner healing. In a prayer led by the priest or the parents, all should pray for the healing of scars caused by traumatic experiences in the womb, during labor, birth, or any time before this moment of Baptism. We might pray: "We know, O Lord, that you love this child and want him/her to be free. May your Spirit now rise within this child of yours and touch all areas of hurt, bringing healing and peace."

At the conclusion, the celebrant calls everyone to pray together and gives a special blessing to the mothers and fathers.

It is truly appropriate for a parish or Christian community to continue to celebrate together in some fashion after the formal rite is completed. Such celebrations where all the parish is welcome can deepen the bonds of Christian love and strengthen the commitment of those gathered.

A significant number of priests have reported that charismatic renewal led them to find significantly deeper life and meaning in this sacrament. May this deepening continue for all of us.

7

Confirmation

Despite great efforts by pastors and catechists, Confirmation remains an obscure sacrament. The Provisional Text of the Revised Rite emphasizes that Confirmation complements Baptism and links with the Eucharist. The three together comprise the sacraments of initiation. For this reason, the Confirmation rite is to begin with the renewal of baptismal promises and be received within the Eucharistic liturgy. While the rite generally anticipates that Confirmation will be conferred about the age of seven, it allows for local custom to delay it. This is the practice in the United States where Confirmation is usually conferred several years after the first communion. This practice has been established so that "the candidate may renew and reaffirm his baptismal commitment with greater awareness of Christian responsibility."*

However, most Catholics recall Confirmation differently. It was a time preceded by weeks of drills in questions and answers about faith. For most, Confirmation was the first time they saw a bishop; a bishop who asked a few questions, slapped them gently on the cheek (a moment preceded by great anxiety), and then told them they were soldiers of Christ. While recent practice has involved more variations and greater

*Rite of Confirmation Provisional Text. NCCB. Bishop's Committee on Liturgy. Washington, D.C., 1972, p. 2.

attempts to replace mystery with understanding, the problem with Confirmation is still with us and can be simply stated: Pastors, teachers, parents, and ultimately those confirmed do not know what is meant by the coming of the Holy Spirit in the sacrament. If this coming is so important, why don't those confirmed experience any change? More directly, why aren't those confirmed treated any differently after Confirmation? If now they are to be witnesses of Christ, performers of apostolic service, why are they not given new apostolic service to do? It is understandable enough that people should have no recollection of being saved, and filled with new life at Baptism, since this happened for most when they were infants. But are Catholics to be sent forth from Confirmation to witness still not knowing any difference?

Theologians rightly state that Baptism and Confirmation are so closely linked that it is impossible to make a clear distinction between them. This then raises the larger question: When do baptized and confirmed Christians know that they are different from non-Christians? When do they know that they are temples of God, filled with the Holy Spirit, strengthened for combat, with their minds enlightened, and possessing spiritual gifts? They know it when they are able to respond to that call in *living* faith. But what is such faith? Faith is not supposed to be a wishfulness or hopefulness but a response such as found in Hebrews: "Faith is confident assurance concerning what we hope for, and conviction about things we do not see" (Heb. 11:1).

Again it is expectant faith which enables us to desire the power of the Spirit, to daily anticipate without disappointment those gifts and graces necessary to live fully Christian lives. In turn we are then enabled to be sisters and brothers and servants to one another.

How can such a faith be nurtured in baptized Christians? What kind of preparation is needed?

The Christian community or local parish needs to have a clear understanding of what will happen in Confirmation. Jesus not only confers the Spirit but brings forth the power of the Holy Spirit, called by some the release of the Spirit or being baptized in the Spirit. The recipient is to know a new presence of Jesus as Risen Lord, a new power to pray, a new strength to speak of his faith, and the beginning of new spiritual gifts ordinarily signified by praying in tongues.

We believe the community, under its pastor, should decide who has sufficient understanding and desire to commit their lives under the lordship of Jesus. We believe those ready should be prepared through a course of study which develops expectant faith, such as the Life in the Spirit Seminars, widely used by Catholic charismatic groups. The current courses tend to develop only dogmatic faith—faith in a series of propositions rather than in a personal relationship with Jesus Christ. We believe that the newly confirmed should be given new responsibilities in prayer, study, and religious service, because they now have new power to discharge these responsibilities. They should daily join their parents in vocal prayer; they should be part of ongoing formation classes; they should be called to serve in a way which is consonant with their gifts in parish life.

The revised rite of Confirmation calls forth the faith commitment of all who are present. The opening prayer of the celebrant has four forms of calling on the Lord to send his Holy Spirit: "to live in our hearts and make us temples of his glory;" "to make us witnesses before the world to the good news;" "to help us walk in unity of faith and grow in the strength of his love;" and "to enlighten our minds and lead us to all truth." God hears and answers our prayers. The assembly should expect these petitions to be granted.

Scripture says that everyone experienced some sign of new life and power through the coming of the Spirit. We can see this in both the scriptural account of the first Pentecost (Acts 2) and the fact that "when St. Paul placed his hands on those who had been baptized, the Holy Spirit came upon them and they began to speak in other languages and prophetic words" (Acts 19:1-7).* Does this fail to happen today because we do not expect it to happen and do not teach others to expect it? We suspect the answer is yes. We know of a few cases where sisters have prepared children for Confirmation with this expectancy. Following their Confirmation, the children spoke of a new feeling that Jesus was in them and a number of them also began praying in tongues. We believe God desires this for all who open themselves in faith to the action of the Spirit. For such persons, we believe that the gifts as specified in Isaiah 11:2 and 1 Cor. 12:4-11 should be operative and manifested in power.

Those to be confirmed are called to renew the profession of faith they made or their parents made for them at Baptism. In the renewal of promises they are asked: "Do you believe in the Holy Spirit, the Lord and giver of life, who came to the apostles at Pentecost and who comes to you today in the Sacrament of Confirmation?"** These are not simply ritual statements or questions. This is the moment when those to be confirmed are called to open in faith to prepare for a new, personal encounter with God in his Holy Spirit.

If those gathered to witness the Confirmation don't believe fully in the above words, they should not participate in the celebration. Most of those being confirmed are young people. When the celebrant, usually the bishop, calls the parish as a whole to confirm the faith just proclaimed by their "Amen," those same young people will know whether that "faith response" comes from the heart or is merely lip service. The

*Rite of Confirmation, p. 20.
**Rite of Confirmation, p. 21.

presence or absence of a faith environment will set the tone for the newly confirmed's Christian life. Therefore, this should be an essential moment in the life of the whole parish, a moment of profession of faith in which "that unity which has the Spirit as its origin" (Eph. 4) is proclaimed and deepened.

Those to be confirmed may make a public statement at this point that they dedicate themselves to the mission of the gospel, to bear witness to the Lord before all the world, and to eagerly work for the building up of the body of Christ. Such declarations can have a powerful beneficial effect on all present and can be stated in the words of those being confirmed. This practice should be followed if at all possible.

The sacrament is actually conferred through the anointing with chrism on the forehead, which is done by the imposition of the hand and through the words, "Receive the seal of the Holy Spirit, the Gift of the Father." This imposition of the hand is not easily seen since it is done in the same action as making the sign of the cross with the thumb on the candidate's forehead. Because this imposition of hands is done in such a subtle manner, it is important that the earlier imposition of hands not be omitted. This occurs just before the anointing with oil. At this time, the ritual prescribes that the bishop extend his hands over all the candidates while praying: "All powerful God, Father of Our Lord Jesus Christ, by water and the Holy Spirit you freed these candidates from sin. Send your Holy Spirit upon them to be their Helper and Guide. Give them the spirit of wisdom and understanding, the spirit of right judgment and courage, the spirit of reverence in your service, through Christ Our Lord."*

This is a powerful prayer and a time of final petition before the anointing with oil and conferral of the sacrament. The congregation should support the bishop in this prayer. It would

*Rite of Confirmation, p. 34.

seem appropriate for the people in the assembly to lift their hands as a sign of common intercession during this prayer.

The oil of chrism used in the anointing both symbolizes and effects new strength of the Spirit in those confirmed. Through this anointing with oil, imposition of hand, and prayer, Jesus encounters each candidate and confirms him or her in the Holy Spirit. The newly confirmed receive an indelible character, the seal of the Lord Jesus, through the gift of the Spirit.

There should be follow-up sessions with the confirmed so that they understand what has happened, what is new in their lives, and what new ways of living they will follow. A good example of such basic teaching is found in the growth seminars and Foundations in Christian Living courses used by prayer groups and communities in the charismatic renewal. These courses deal with such topics as:

-Personal prayer
-Sacraments and worship
-Use of gifts in communal prayer and service
-Growth in spiritual life
-Personality and emotional growth
-Forgiveness and reconciliation
-Christian role in social justice
-Vocational discernment

We recommend that these and similar topics constitute the material of the follow-up sessions for the newly confirmed. Ideally, after the first year of instruction, an in-depth study of the material suggested above should be incorporated into ongoing high school and adult education programs in the parish.

The final point concerns sponsors. Past practice frequently had one man sponsor all the boys and one woman sponsor the girls. In my own Confirmation, I (Fr. M.) never met the man who was my sponsor and saw him from a distance only on the day of Confirmation. The revised rite suggests that the god-parents from Baptism be the sponsors. This seems to be an excellent practice since it links the two sacraments and deepens the relationship of godparents and sponsors. It should also be clear that the Christian community is sponsoring the candidates. The community or parish should be called to stand behind the sponsor and be committed to support the newly confirmed. It would also seem preferable to have the sponsors and godparents come from the same parish as the confirmed, since this is the primary community for the one to be confirmed. In this way, the sponsor can more directly guide and support the one confirmed. At present, this ideal will probably give way to many practical considerations, such as the parents' desire to have family members who live at a distance serve in the role. In any case, it is vitally important that sponsors understand the gravity of the commitment they make to God and to the one being confirmed.

This analysis of Confirmation may seem to place heavy demands upon those who will attempt to follow the recommendations. We refer the reader again to Chapter 3. All the recommendations will be difficult to introduce to the extent that the Church is not already being celebrated.

Let us be practical. None of what has been written in this chapter can be developed unless those to be confirmed have been growing in a supportive community. Most Christians lack this supportive community. In many parishes, Sunday liturgy is the only time people meet; for most, the meeting consists of sitting next to nameless strangers. Community is a word in these parishes which carries no life, no power.

In parishes, those who work on committees or serve the people in some capacity often begin to find fellowship in these groups. Yet even here there is often dissension, rivalry, and gossip, and the pastor ends up in an energy-draining role of mediator. It is true that some parishes have formed community and have begun to understand in their life together the Spirit as the bond of unity and peace as its binding force (Eph. 4:3). But such parishes are few in number.

What needs to happen?

In order for Church to be celebrated and, therefore, the sacrament of Confirmation to come alive, we need to take some basic steps in our personal and parish life:

1. We need to experience how deeply we are loved by God and what God desires to do in our lives with power.

2. In the power of that love, each person needs to experience that personal conversion of heart, to turn again to the Lord, renounce sin, accept his lordship, and live in the grace-filled responsibility of our baptismal call.

3. We need to experience God's healing love in our personal difficulties as well as in reconciliation with one another.

4. In the light of God's love and word, we need to establish priorities in our lives: family, our work, service to Church and civic community.

5. Out of these priorities, we need to see what commitment of presence and service God desires we make to one another in the parish or Christian community.

6. This commitment to our brothers and sisters, in addition to personal conversion, is essential for the formation of and our own participation in a worshipping, celebrating community.

7. We need to know in the Sunday liturgy that we can celebrate in word and Eucharist what God has already done in our lives. In the strength of that truth we can then respond to the next step which God makes known to us in Word and sacrament.

That is the beginning of community.

Unless each parish comes to terms with who it is before God, unless we begin to realize the enormity of God's merciful love calling us to partake of a plan far beyond our meager hopes for our lives and families, all the forms of renewal, new rites and programs will be nothing more than a house built on a foundation of sand. Words like community, covenant, reconciliation will be nothing more than *now* words, fad words, shadows of the bedrock foundation of God's truth, echoes which will fade away, devoid of power to effect change.

We do not speak to condemn or to burden beyond the ability to bear, for the way to the light does not depend on our strength. So many have labored for the truth and been burned out, exhausted by the obstacles. What God wants us to know is that the power comes from him and not from us. We need to learn how to be open to that power. We need to know we can call on it, expect it, rely on it. We need to experience the great *hope* to which we are called (Eph. 1:18). God holds out that power to us, especially thorugh the graces of Baptism and Confirmation. His love which brings those graces is constant and faithful.

We can speak only to call us all to face the truth of where we are. Once that is acknowledged and we cry as a people for his mercy and strength, we will be given power *as we have not known it before*.

Then Confirmation makes sense. A community sees the gifts it needs, nurtures them in one another, supports the life of one another. The community becomes a body of love and so Confirmation becomes a mutual gift. The one confirmed rejoices in his gifts, sees his place to serve in the body. He knows how God desires to use him, knows his value, rejoices that he is wanted, needed, confirmed. In turn, the community is gifted more deeply because it is enriched and strengthened through another sister or brother who desires to give her/his life in service.

8

The Eucharist

We have referred to the Eucharist in the early chapters of this book and have used it as the primary model for sacraments coming alive. Consequently, we would now like to discuss this sacrament in a more narrow perspective.

The Eucharist is the solemn rite of worship for the Christian community. It is the time for the community to join with Jesus in worshipping the Father in the power of the Spirit. Jesus thanks the Father for all of salvation history. As High Priest and Risen Lord, he intercedes for us at the right hand of the Father. We join with Jesus in the paschal mystery of his death, resurrection, and glorification and we are called into mystery far behind our comprehension. We can only step forward in faith and become part of actions which transcend all that is ordinary and proper to our lives.

However, the very importance of the Eucharist means we must approach it in a balanced way. We need to approach it in a fashion which is consistent with the exalted nature of the liturgy and yet does not call us beyond a level where we can be meaningfully present, where we can celebrate with our lives. Therefore, we will not multiply the rich theological considerations already so well developed in many books but instead simply pinpoint what has worked in our lives to bring forth meaning. To accomplish this, we will speak from two points of view. Each of us will describe the power of a eucharistic celebration when those gathered recognize and expect the power of the Spirit to transform and renew. We will also each reflect from our unique perspectives on the ways our openness and approach to the eucharistic celebration can help make God's power more fully present.

I (Fr. M.) will take the perspective of the disciples who recognized Jesus in the breaking of the bread. Their eyes were opened and then they recalled that their hearts were burning within them when Jesus explained the Scriptures. The following account attempts to describe what caused my heart to burn within me and my eyes to be opened so that I recognized Jesus in a new way in the Eucharist.

My life has centered about the Eucharist for many years, but especially since my ordination to the priesthood in 1964. I remember the details of my first mass I celebrated on the day after ordination. I remember fondly the mass for my brother's wedding and the masses following my mother's and father's deaths. It was a grand privilege to offer the Eucharist at these key moments.

I remember the joy of the Eucharist first being celebrated in English. There was great excitement and a new sense of community with the congregation. Before this time, I had been very aware of the tremendous mystery but barely aware of my brothers and sisters in the congregation once the liturgy of the Word was completed.

I remember the significance of the first masses with civil rights themes. We thrilled to new folk music such as "We Shall Overcome," and read Martin Luther King's speech, "I Have a Dream." Then the poor people's march and the peace movement were occasions for special masses. The Cursillo movement introduced me to a new relationship to Jesus as brother. I anticipated with joy each opportunity to celebrate the Eucharist with my fellow cursillistas.

Later, it was an important moment in my life when I returned to the seminary, now as rector, and was able to preside at some well-prepared celebrations. The seminary liturgies combined the best in music, full congregational singing, well-developed and delivered homilies, and rich symbolism.

However, in the summer of 1969, I began to know a new hunger within me. I prayed that God would fill the restless void in my heart. In the next few months I felt an immediate call to holiness. I felt a new need to be more fully a priest in imitation of Jesus. I knew my prayer life had to assume new importance. I hungered for what could meet these needs; I wondered where I would find the answer. A Carmelite Sister and then a seminarian told me about "the baptism in the Spirit."* I didn't need more than a brief explanation. I knew this was it; I needed to be filled with the Holy Spirit. Somehow, though I knew the Trinity dwelt within me, I also knew that the Spirit of God had to take over in the center of my life. I needed power from within. So I researched this "baptism of the Spirit." I studied the Scriptures and read the testimonies of those who had experienced it. I knew a growing desire to commit my life more than ever before under the lordship of Jesus. I waited for my opportunity to be baptized in the Spirit.

In October 1969, a priest and a young graduate student from Fordham came to Saint Francis College in Loretto, Pennsylvania, to give a talk on this baptism and a new way of knowing Jesus. They prayed that evening that Jesus might baptize me in his Spirit. It happened. I was immediately caught up in prayer. I knew an intimate presence of God. I knelt in the center of the room for a considerable time, conscious only of God's presence. I would so easily have cried out with Peter: "Lord let us build three tents here." Eventually, someone touched me and I got up, walked to a corner of the room and sat there for

---

*While the term "release of the Spirit" is more theologically accurate, at the time of these events, the only term in use was "baptism in the Spirit."

maybe another hour. I was doing nothing. God had grasped me. There were no words, no thoughts, just a presence, just an experience of glory. Someone asked me to pray for another priest that he might grow in wisdom. I moved over to where he was kneeling. I started to pray, asking Jesus to give him this gift. As I began speaking, my tongue moved in new ways and different sounds came out of me. I was not saying the English words I was thinking. So I stopped speaking. (The movement of the sounds but without voice continued within me.) I sensed I was thanking the Father for the gift I received. I sensed I was praising God for his goodness.

That night I went quickly to sleep. Many times during that night I awoke and discovered that the prayer was still going on in me. I had not decided to pray, but prayer was going on: It was a prayer of praise to the Father. It was almost as if I were a spectator, but it was going on in me and through me.

The next morning, I experienced an overwhelming desire to read Scripture. I read the Acts of the Apostles. It seemed the words had new life and power to touch me. I saw new meaning. I sensed that I was in the Acts as one of the disciples of Jesus. The Acts seemed not so much a document of the past but words about today and for today. I had to discipline myself to stop reading and praying after two hours had passed.

I went to my office. I knew I wanted to go back to reading Scripture, but I dictated letters instead. About 11:00 a.m., I decided to write down what I was experiencing. I wrote: "I know Jesus living within me as the Risen Lord Jesus." This summarized it—I was experiencing Jesus in glory, Jesus with risen life. I checked my emotions and there was little excitement; the experience was deeper than that. Jesus was there in a new way beneath or beyond my feelings.

I went to the chapel to celebrate the Eucharist with the priests and seminarians who had been with me the night before. The Eucharist was different. I experienced being led through the penitential rite. It seemed the Holy Spirit was showing me new areas for repentance. I knew a deep sorrow for being unfaithful in so many ways. The sorrow was quickly replaced with a new power to praise as we began "Glory to God." I noticed a oneness among us as we praised God together. The words of the Epistle and Gospel were like personal messages to me. They seemed to touch my heart and began to change me. I had the sense of receiving a personal message about my life. We all commented on the homily and I was amazed that each of us seemed to be responding the same way. We acknowledged our own sinful nature and rejoiced that Jesus was our Savior and Lord.

As we entered the Canon of the Mass, I was caught up in a body with my brothers; I knew for the first time that Jesus was offering us as his body to the Father. That was an extraordinary moment. I had known about this truth, but now I was in it. We sang the Our Father as an anthem. We embraced with a new sense of oneness at the kiss of peace and dwelt silently together with a new unity following communion. That is all I remember about that Eucharist.

I thought this Eucharist might be a peak experience never to be relived, but this was not so. I have participated in many, many powerful liturgies since. I have learned much about how to celebrate, but the most important thing I have learned is that we celebrate in the Spirit. It is the Holy Spirit who cries within us, "Abba, Father." It is that Spirit who leads the repentance, praise, Scripture proclamation and response, and the sacrifice of Jesus to the Father. I have learned what to do to yield to the Spirit, how to remove blocks to the Spirit, how to help others to yield and join with me. I respect the desires of many good and holy people who do not want to join in this celebrating of liturgy in the Spirit, but I eagerly anticipate those special times when everyone present knows that the Spirit can lead our celebration and wants it to happen.

When I am presiding at a liturgy where those present are open to this way of celebrating the liturgy with the Spirit, I usually make the following special efforts. They have helped me and many of my brother priests serve better as celebrants.

1. I begin with praise in song and prayer. This leads everyone to center on God and to forget themselves. This also leads them to experience a unity with one another.

2. From the vantage point of praise, I ask those present to let the Spirit reveal to them in the Penitential Rite whatever is blocking their closer union with God and their freedom to offer themselves to the Father in this liturgy. For example, I did this in October 1975 as the principal celebrant at a closing liturgy for approximately 5,000 persons attending the Upper Midwest Charismatic Conference. There followed a series of prophecies. Three people came to the microphone in succession to speak of the Lord's desire to purify us with his love. We followed that word and knew in our hearts in concrete ways a reconciliation with God and one another for sins of pride and insensitivity as indicated by the prophecies.

3. Following the Penitential Rite, I usually try to lead a song or prayer praising God's glory. I find that the deeper the people go within to be purified, the more fully they can subsequently give themselves in praise. When appropriate, I lead the people into praying and singing in the prayer language of tongues. At a number of liturgies in charismatic conferences, I have led an extended period of praise and song before the liturgy of the Word.

4. The Word of God is meant to be proclaimed in the liturgy. I believe that the congregation deserves to hear it proclaimed. Therefore, I attempt to get the best possible readers and have them prepared to proclaim. I do not use those who mumble, read fast, do not appreciate Scripture, or cannot surrender to the power of the Word.

5. I see that there is a pause for reflection and prayer

following each proclamation of Scripture. Sometimes it is appropriate here to give a mini-homily after the Old Testament or New Testament reading, if this will prepare people to be more open to the gospel proclamation.

6. I particularly try to see that the gospel is proclaimed as good news and that the homily accentuates the good news of the Scripture that has been proclaimed. I believe that the power of the Scriptures should flow directly into the power of the homily. The congregation should experience the two as one. I don't think the homily should be a detached reflection on Scripture or a preaching primarily on some Scriptures other than the ones proclaimed. The members of the congregation should sense that the message of Scripture is being made a relevant word with specific application to today. They should be able to respond affirmatively, accepting that word for themselves in their lives at this time, and rejoicing that there is good news because Jesus came. The homily needs to be news, something new and fresh. It needs to be good, something that may convict and challenge people but which clearly leads to a better life. I have heard and at times have given sermons which can best be described as bad repetition. They repeated what people had heard before and they left them with a sense that their lives and situations in society were discouraging if not hopeless.

To me, the most important aspect of Scripture is its sacramentality; that is, it is a means of encountering Christ and therefore God in Christ. Scripture is inspired, that is, "breathed into" by the Holy Spirit. Because the power of the Spirit is in the words of Scripture, those words have the power to touch the spirit in me in a way which no other words can. This sacramentality is an effect of the inspiration of Scripture. Most scholarly studies on the inspiration of Scripture concentrate on inerrancy or the quality of not being in error. This, too, is an effect of inspiration, but it is stated in negative terms.

The positive quality of inspiration is sacramentality, which means the quality of meeting Jesus—the Word of God—in the words of Scripture. It is the quality that gives power to the homily. So many people comment that after being baptized in the Spirit they couldn't quench the desire to read Scripture. Their spirits were alive to the Spirit in the Word. The homily should draw the spirit within those present so that the good news is alive in them. The homily is the fuse between the fire of the word and the spirit of the people. Regardless of the nature of the homily, it should bring the congregation to the response that "truly the kingdom of God is at hand."

7. The time after the homily should be a time of reflection and response where appropriate. If the homily has been delivered in power, the people want to pause and dwell with it. If the liturgy is being celebrated with a congregation that is comfortable with charismatic word gifts, someone will frequently give a brief word that confirms and endorses the message of the homily. The word may be given in many forms such as a prophetic word which comes from God in a special way, in the form of a short teaching, or as an insight that could be called a word of wisdom.

8. The Creed should express the full response of the congregation that it believes what has been proclaimed. With the right exhortation, the congregation will recite the creed in a fresh and faith-filled way.

9. The petitions can be an experience of power or frustration. It is deadening to hear a list of prepared petitions read in an apathetic fashion. The petitions should be pertinent to the day and expressed with spontaneous freshness and some urgency. It is frustrating to hear petitions which encompass every need people can think of because it is usually difficult to pray for all the ills of the world. It is easier to pray for the people whose needs somehow flow from the content of the homily. It is easier to pray for people and situations that di-

rectly relate to our lives and the lives of others present. It seems preferable for individuals to pray for their "special intentions" as part of a general prayer instead of mentioning them out loud. I usually ask the congregation to pause in prayer and mention other needs they sense the Lord wants them to bring to the awareness of all. When one of these spontaneous petitions seems to have special urgency or evokes an immediate response of the congregation, I stop and have those present pray specifically for it before proceeding with other petitions.

10. The Offertory is most effective when it provides many ways in which those present can offer themselves to the Father. The Offertory is a time for offering the gifts of the liturgy, the monetary substance of life, and the very lives of those present. If the people can come forward to the altar, this action can well symbolize such an offering. It also can express the entrance into the holy of holies for the more solemn moments of the liturgy. Music which calls forth the offering of ourselves is most appropriate.

11. The Preface is a call to oneness and raising all to God. "Lift up your hearts" should be expressed as a call to action. If the people hear it, they will respond forcefully, "We lift them up to the Lord." "Let us give thanks to the Lord our God" should express real intention to give thanks. The people will then reply, "It is right to give him thanks and praise" in a way that encourages all *to do just that*. The words of the Preface proper can then carry forth in that spirit and evoke a fervent "Holy, Holy, Holy," preferably in song.

12. The Eucharistic Prayer is solemn—a time of reverential silence and awesome mystery. All actions should foster this meaning. I find that the daily repetition of the prescribed words of the Eucharistic Prayer adds to their meaning as long as the awesomeness of the time is maintained.

13. At the conclusion of the Eucharistic Prayer, the

celebrant proclaims the words, "Through him, with him and in him in the unity of the Holy Spirit, all honor and glory is yours, Almighty Father." If it is proclaimed out of living faith, as a final triumphant note to the Eucharistic Prayer, the people will respond with understanding and power in their "Amen."

14. The ritual calls for the main celebrant to invite those present to join as brothers and sisters, redeemed by the Lord, to acknowledge our common Father. To the extent that the congregation knows this unity, they will be able to pray with a lively faith.

15. The Kiss of Peace can take many forms. There are different signs of peace such as handshaking, embracing, kissing, and holding hands. Whatever sign is used, it should flow from the power of the liturgy and lead to a prayerful reception of the body and blood of the Lord. It should not interrupt the liturgy for a social time nor should it be a series of empty gestures and routine actions.

16. The main celebrant and the congregation say special healing prayers before Communion. The celebrant, in the first of his prayers, says, "Lord Jesus Christ, with faith in your love and mercy I eat your body and drink your blood. Let it not bring me condemnation but health in mind and body." The people proclaim, "Lord, I am not worthy to receive you, but only say the word and I shall be healed." These prayers should be recited with expectant faith that the Lord wants to heal us and in his love for us will do so. The celebrant may have to instruct the people in the importance of these prayers.

17. "There is one Lord, one faith, one baptism and one God and Father of all" (Eph. 4:5-6). This oneness in the Lord is the key to receiving Jesus as really present, sacramentally, in the bread and wine. We are to be one with Jesus and through him one with the Father in the Spirit. We are to be one with our brothers and sisters in this presence. Wounds of disunity and alienation are to be healed through the power of this pres-

ence. The Church Fathers called the Eucharist the ordinary sacrament of healing. There should be time to dwell conscious of that presence and time to receive healing, grasping it in faith. The celebrant should see that a spirit of peace prevails. As much as possible, any flurry of activity, even in purifying patens and chalices should be avoided. In settings where there is openness to charismatic word gifts, this is the most likely time to receive words of love, encouragement, and calling to go forth in servant love. The presiding celebrant should listen carefully to what is happening and to the leadings of the Spirit within him to determine how long this period should be. Music which undergirds the reflection and prayer should be encouraged.

18. The final prayer, blessing, and sending forth are very important. They should not be treated as routine endings. At the end of any meeting where very significant events have taken place, the chairman of the meeting will make reference to these and dismiss the meeting in the same spirit in which it has taken place. So, in the liturgy, the president of the assembly—the presiding celebrant—should convey the meaning of the liturgy. The sending forth should partake of the same spirit that is present in the final words of Matthew's Gospel: "Go therefore, and make disciples of all the nations; baptize them in the name of the Father and of the Son and of the Holy Spirit. Teach them to carry out everything I have commanded you. And know that I am with you always; until the end of the world" (Matt. 28:19-20).

(Sr. A.): Father Michael has reflected on the liturgy which is truly celebrated in power and the enduring fruit it can produce in all our lives. Many of us have experienced such a liturgical celebration and can identify with the truth of Father's personal reflections.

However, such a eucharistic celebration, while realistically possible and desirable, is nevertheless a rare experience for most at this time. Thus how can we "tap into" the power of the liturgy and the Eucharist itself when the congregation is not living in expectant faith, when its members do not know that the Lord wants to touch their lives in a new way each time they gather for the eucharistic celebration?

No celebration of the Eucharist should be a "God and me" experience. Therefore, when I am not with those who are united in *expectant* faith, I "take concern" before mass for those gathered. That is, I pray that whatever burdens or anxieties they are carrying may be lifted so that they can hear his word and receive him with new awareness.

At the penitential rite, I ask God's forgiveness for anyone in the group I may have offended which could block or hinder their openness to God and their brothers and sisters.

Immediately before the liturgy of the Word, I pray that those reading may gain a new insight from even one line of Scripture so that the fire of God's word may begin to burn in them and they will one day be able to proclaim his word with power. In the same way I pray that my own heart will be touched each time.

Before the homily begins, I always ask God to refresh the priest (who may have had to celebrate three masses already that weekend) so that he may not see the homily as a burden but as an opportunity to shepherd his people more care-fully. I pray that whatever distractions are the people's at that time, the word may penetrate in power and we will all, priest and people, respond to God and one another in the truth of that word.

In the Prayer of the Faithful, I first remember in my heart all those at this mass whose burdens are so deep and faith so shattered that they cannot lift them to the Lord. Then I pray quietly in tongues as all the other petitions are read.

At the Kiss of Peace, I pray that by genuinely offering peace even to those around me whom I may not know, I can extend an infinite gift by consciously making it a faith-filled gesture. In that way it is possible to be an instrument whereby others may begin to open to that peace which surpasses all understanding.

Before the reception of the Eucharist, I try to consciously pray in the name of all the people, "Say but the word and I shall be healed."

In the first part of my thanksgiving after the Eucharist, I ask God to heal all those gathered with me, to allow that healing to begin by letting them know God as a God of love, to have new hope.

I believe God responds to that kind of prayer. I believe when I pray that way I am also more open to how he wants me to relate and act with these people outside the eucharistic celebration. I believe that when people pray privately in their hearts this way, a gradual transformation will take place. A parish will be reborn in faith and our own hearts will burn within us!

For the past year, I have been privileged to be part of the Renewal Center community at The College of Steubenville in Ohio. I am able to participate daily in a eucharistic liturgy which is celebrated in power and with full use of charismatic gifts. For me the greatest blessing has been a living awareness of being part of the body of Christ. To experience in power the richness of his gifts in my sisters and brothers, to share in the reception of his body and blood as part of a repentant and hungry people has enabled bonds of love and trust to be established which are beyond the power of words.

I see weakness acknowledged, forgiveness given, support found.

I see gifts of wisdom and understanding, of prophecy and words of knowledge called forth, proclaimed, and confirmed in power.

I see lives transformed because through the eucharistic celebration people are convicted by the word of Scripture: repent and know new healing and life in the daily reception of his body and blood.

Together as a people we know the truth of Peter's words and can celebrate it:

> . . . You are a chosen race, a royal priesthood, a consecrated nation, a people set apart to sing the praises of God who called you out of the darkness into his wonderful light. Once you were not a people at all and now you are the People of God; once you were outside the mercy and now you have been given mercy.
>
> (1 Pet. 2:9-10, Jerusalem Bible)

God desires all his people to experience that reality so that, in truth, we may be his body—so that his kingdom may come.

Wherever we are, however we gather to celebrate the body and blood of the Lord, let this be our prayer.

9

Anointing of the Sick

Most people still respond awkwardly to the mention of the sacrament of the Anointing of the Sick. If a priest visits a home to anoint a sick person, he encounters a blend of awe, awkwardness, and confusion. Most see the sacrament as good for the dying but they shun any personal part in it. They tend to see the sacrament as a solemn farewell, a necessary evil. This attitude has changed somewhat with the change in the name of the sacrament from Extreme Unction to Anointing of the Sick, and with the greater latitude of using the sacrament for any serious illness, for the aged, and in conjunction with the Sunday liturgy.

What needs to happen is that the good news of the healing power of Jesus be proclaimed to all. In the Anointing of the Sick we meet the healing Jesus just as the deaf, dumb, blind, and leprous met him in Palestine. Not everyone who receives the sacrament is restored to physical health, but everyone is offered the most loving thing the Lord can give them. The most loving response may in fact be a peaceful preparation for passage to heaven.

Our personal experience has included the following:

-A man dying of malaria recovered within 24 hours after being anointed (see *Inner Healing,* Paulist Press, 1974, p. 6).

-A woman suffering from a stroke was unconcious and not

able to respond to stimuli. I (Fr. M.) administered the sacrament of Anointing while the family joined in the prayer for healing. Two days later I received a call from the family to report an amazingly quick recovers. Their mother was home and doing fine.

-An elderly sister troubled with a severe back problem for many years was anointed during a particularly painful siege. She had suffered such pain for many years, and would frequently be confined to her bed for three to four days at a time. This time, after the anointing, she was immediately freed of the pain and had no recurrence for 18 months.

-A sister was scheduled for open heart surgery. Her doctor had indicated he could not operate if her anxiety and tension were not greatly reduced. During the Anointing of the Sick, some members of the Christian community gathered with her to pray. After the surgery the doctor thanked *her* for the privilege of operating on her heart for he said "it was so peaceful and firm."

-The most touching case involved a completely paralyzed girl in a hospital for the incurably ill and dying in Brisbane, Australia. She had been unable to respond in any way following an automobile accident six months before. She was twisted out of shape. The doctors indicated that her mental condition was that of a vegetable. A group of us prayed. After the Anointing we spoke in her ear about God's love for her, about who was present, about how we cared and were praying for her. Then we asked her to try and squeeze our hands if she understood anything we had said. With her twisted hands she squeezed our hands, stretched her misshapen and shrunken body full length on the bed, sighed and began to cry. It was the first communication from her since the accident.

-On the other hand, there was one striking case of a terminally ill woman who was terribly anxious about her own death. She was in her forties and had a number of young children. She spoke to me (Fr. M.) of her great fear of leaving them and her husband. After receiving the sacrament great peace enveloped her. She told me she was all right and suggested I visit other patients who might need me. The next day, she died, and her family has been well cared for.

-Sixty-two priests at the National Priests Conference reported witnessing healings in the sacrament of Anointing. One priest commented: "Since I have discovered that the effect of the sacrament is to heal, I have witnessed healings. For the first 26 years of my priesthood, I didn't know God did that."

In the actual Anointing of the Sick it should be clear that this is *not* a matter just between the priest and the sick person. Indeed, in James 5, the injunction is:

> Is there anyone sick among you? He should ask for the presbyters of the church. They in turn are to pray over him anointing him with oil in the Name [of the Lord]. This prayer uttered in faith will reclaim the one who is ill, and the Lord will restore him to health. If he has committed any sins, forgiveness will be his.
>
> (James 5:14-15)

By mentioning the presbyters or elders, Scripture implicitly calls the body of mature believers to join in prayer, for it is the prayer in faith which reclaims the ill person. Therefore, we emphasize the importance, when at all possible, for a people of faith to gather in supportive prayer during the Anointing of the Sick.

The revised rite of Anointing makes provision for this general participation in the sacrament. The priest is directed, when possible, to open with a greeting of peace and then to sprinkle the sick and the room with holy water. He then addresses all present, reading from James 5. The priest must choose between one prayer which asks "that the Lord may ease his/her suffering and grant him/her health and salvation,'' and another which asks, ''protect our brother or our sister in his/her illness. Lead us all to the peace and joy of your kingdom where you live for ever and ever.'' The Church is putting the obligation on the priest to decide whether to pray specifically for healing by using the first prayer. In making such a decision, we believe the priest should ordinarily pray for healing specifically and only use the second prayer if he has overriding evidence that the Lord probably intends this illness to end in death.

There follows a penitential rite to be participated in by all. This is followed by a Scripture reading. The preferred text is Matthew 8:5-13 concerning the healing of the centurion's servant. Some of the alternate Scriptures do not involve healing but rather the promise of reward for faithful service and bearing hardship.

Following the Scripture reading is a litany of petitions. The priest then lays hands on the head of the sick person in silence. Sometimes the laying on of hands is a prayer of faith without any experience of power. Other times the priest may experience power floiing through his hands into the sick person. There may be an extraordinary sense of heat or electricity, or the hands seem to be passing down through the head to the person. These are signs frequently given to encourage us to continue and intensify our prayer. The priest should be willing to spend time in silent prayer or quiet prayer in tongues at this point.

Next the priest prays a prayer of thanksgiving over the oil of the sick, saying in part, ''You humbled yourself to share in our humanity, and you desired to cure all our illnesses.'' This is an amazing statement by the Church that Jesus desired to cure not just some but all our illnesses.

At the completion of the prayer, the priest anoints the sick person with the oil on the forehead and hands saying:

"Through this holy anointing may the Lord in his love and mercy help you with the grace of the Holy Spirit. R. Amen. May the Lord who frees you from sin save you and raise you up. R. Amen."

There follow five alternatives for the final prayer. Two of these prayers pray for healing, two are general prayers, and one states that the sick person is about to die. The priest again must choose. He should again choose the healing prayer in the absence of contrary evidence regarding God's will.

The supportive prayer of those assembled should be the strongest prayer in faith that they are capable of offering. In some circumstances, this will include praying and singing in tongues, raising hands, and extending hands over the sick person. It aids the prayer for all to know the nature of the illness and to focus on that. Use of prophecy or Scripture passages for this purpose should be carefully tested by those with confirmed gifts of discernment before being proclaimed. Further, those testing and exercising a word gift should in all probability be people outside the immediate family circle of the sick person. It is so easy to be misled in these emotional circumstances, especially when we are bound by ties of love to the sick person. To proclaim a word as from the Lord which in actuality is more from our own needs and desires can cause unnecessary grief and even mockery of spiritual gifts.

The celebration of the sacrament should conclude with praise to the Lord for his never-ending love and care. The length and volume of this praise should be appropriate to the condition of the sick person and the private or public setting in which we are praying. Certainly we have more freedom to express our faith in a private home than we would in a hospital where sensitivity to the illness of others must be of primary importance.

The prayer should not end with the sacrament. There should be an ongoing prayer afterward, building on what has already transpired. We know that some diseases seem to be healed over a period of time and that some people take much longer than others to respond to healing. The sick person should be encouraged to state anything he or she truly believes. If within his spirit he knows healing has taken place, then he should be encouraged to claim the healing and thank God for it. If he has no such knowledge, he should not be pressed into saying it is so.

We believe it is equally important to realize that God in his mysterious plan calls some women and men to redemptive suffering; that is, God asks some to suffer physically in this world as part of his plan to bring all men and women to live in the fullness of the redemption wrought by Jesus Christ.

This redemptive suffering is suffering imposed on us by others. It is martyrdom, torture, banishment, enslavement of Christians, and ridicule and deprivation of rights because of one's faith in Christ. Redemptive suffering is also the hardships borne for the sake of the gospel: hunger, cold, shipwreck, and other such sufferings. It is trials and difficulties which strengthen faith and purify hearts. These forms of suffering were borne by Jesus and his disciples. They are the highest forms of worship of the Father, and all Christians are called to bear these crosses. These sufferings can be included in the meaning of Paul's statement to the Christians at Colossae. "Even now I find my joy in the suffering I endure for you. In my own flesh I fill up what is lacking in the sufferings of Christ for the sake of his body, the Church" (Col. 1:24).

Nevertheless, sickness of the body is often difficult to understand. There is no indication that Jesus suffered this way. However, Paul and others did seem to undergo sickness without there being a mention of God healing them. There is also a long history of Christian saints who bore sickness as expressions of love of God and as prayers of reparation and intercession for others. On the other hand, there is a strong tendency in Catholic tradition to normally see sickness as something sent by God and to be borne stoically despite the negative effects it might have on the individual's personality and the welfare of those about him.

How can this be reconciled with our belief that God wants to heal? We believe the answer must be: (1) to always believe in God's desire and power to do the most loving thing; (2) to constantly look for the curing of sickness through bodily resources, medical science, and the Lord's healing power; (3) to be alert for those special instances where sickness is present for the greater good of building up the body of Jesus Christ.

Discernment is needed here. If the person experiencing prolonged suffering is distraught, embittered, or withdrawn, it is obvious that God wants to bring about some kind of change of heart, and we usually need to pray for that first. But, if the suffering person is showing the fruit of the Spirit—love, joy, peace, patience, etc., as outlined in Galatians 5:22—then this is a discernible sign that God's love and power are already present. While we should certainly not be closed to physical healing in such cases, we should realize that perhaps we should pray in this sacrament for a deeper release of God's peace and strength to enable that woman or man to live out God's plan for them of redemptive suffering. Those who minister to such a person usually find themselves immeasurably blessed and enriched by the peace surpassing all understanding which flows from the physically sick man or woman.

We have emphasized the importance of healing in the sacrament of Anointing as well as in other sacraments. We want to state clearly that gifts and ministries of healing are not confined to the sacraments. There are desirable and valuable ways in which people should come together to pray for one another's healings. This is especially true among members of the same family, the same household, or the same prayer group. It would be a mistake to stop praying for healings in these circumstances on the basis that healings occur only in the sacraments. Many persons have experienced physical as well as inner healing through this type of prayer ministry. (We would refer the reader to Francis MacNutt, *Healing*, Ave Maria Press, 1974, for examples and explanations.)

In the light of these experiences we can see the importance of the following statement from the Vatican II Constitution on the Church:

> It is not only through the sacraments and Church ministries that the same Holy Spirit sanctifies and leads the People of God and enriches it with virtues. Alloting his gifts "to everyone as he will" (1 Cor. 12:11), he distributes special graces among the faithful of every rank. By these gifts he makes them fit and ready to undertake the various tasks or offices advantageous for the renewal and upbuilding of the Church according to the words of the Apostle: "The manifestation of the Spirit is given to everyone for profit" (1 Cor. 12:7). These charismatic gifts, whether they be the most outstanding or the more simple and widely diffused, are to be received with thanksgiving and consolation, for they are exceedingly suitable and useful for the needs of the Church.*

In summary, we have seen the many forms of suffering and many ways of healing. We rejoice that the Lord with his healing power is present in the Church and is solemnly encountered in the Sacrament of Anointing. As we attempt to learn all the hows, whens, and whys of his healing power, we find ourselves called more and more deeply to prayer and to the responsibility, in the power of the Spirit, to put on the mind of Christ. We "test everything; retain what is good. Avoid every semblance of evil" (1 Thess. 5:19).

*Abbott (ed.). *op. cit.*, paragraph 12, p. 30.

Whatever the situation may be, whenever we approach the sick we should pray: "Lord, love through me. Give me your compassionate heart; let me see the person as you see him; let me believe that you died for him and want only the best for him. Lord, lead me to do only what you would have me do." It is after such a prayer that we can discern how to reach out and how to pray for healing. The Lord's love is the key to the Anointing of the Sick. For we can be certain that healing will take place: either unto the fullness of kingdom life or for this world as part of the signs and wonders of the kingdom.

10

Matrimony and Orders

Matrimony and Orders can be best understood by considering them together. Traditionally these have been known as the social sacraments because they are directly related to the roles Christians have in common. It is their very communal nature which enlightens the understanding of their power. Therefore, we will highlight the presence or absence of this communal nature by comparing parallel situations in the two sacraments. Consequently, there will be a pattern of frequent alternation in the following discussion.

At the outset we can easily see that these two sacraments stand in the problem spotlight today because of the high incidence of divorce and, in recent years, the significant number of departures from the priesthood. Issues of birth control and abortion are linked to an understanding of Matrimony. In the priesthood, the issues of celibacy and the ordination of women are current problems.

What, fundamentally, is not working in these sacraments? We believe that the basic problem lies in a separation of these sacraments from the basic Christian community which is to be served by the sacraments. The root problem in Matrimony is that the marriage is not proposed out of the life of a Christian community. It lacks the right guidance of the leaders of that community, and lacks the commitment of the whole community to support the marriage and make it work. Instead, marriage has become an isolated affair of two people who decide to marry and then attempt alone to make the marriage work. This places excessive burdens on the married couple for the material and spiritual well-being of the family. It also causes the husband and wife to focus all their emotional needs on each other. Tension, anxiety, and fear grow when needs are not or cannot be met. Often the prospect of adding another child to such a situation becomes something to be avoided at all costs.

The root problem in the priesthood today is similar. The priest experiences an alienation similar to that of the isolated couple. He has been proposed as a candidate for the priesthood basically only by the vocation director. He is sent to a seminary removed from his home parish and the parish he will serve as a priest. After at least four years of study, including some ministry experience somewhere in the diocese, he is assigned to a parish. He comes as the assistant pastor, is usually young and inexperienced, and except for his title of priest, he is one of the last persons the people of the parish would naturally go to for counsel. The people of the parish have had no part in selecting him or in any way discerning whether the Lord was calling him to be a shepherd to them. They made no commitment to accept or support him at his ordination; in turn the priest sees the people as indistinguishable from everyone else in the diocese.

In these circumstances it is no wonder that this priest frequently feels alone, isolated, and living without intimacy in his life. His pastor has worked through the same problems he has and has adjusted some 20 years ago. The people are good to him, but the priest's relationship to them tends to be as a functionary, one who gives service. The priest can experience a drying up of his warmth as a man. He does not need more compliments; he gets too many unfounded or misplaced compliments as it is. He needs people who care about the inside of his life, who correct him and share in the responsibility for his life. And the priest needs to be that for others. Who cares about his prayer life, the relationships he is developing, how he spends his money, or his vacations?

What needs to happen in these sacraments? Basically, they need to flow from an involved Christian community or a parish living a covenant commitment. Within such a community, those in marriage and Holy Orders need to find and give support. The married couple and the community should make explicit commitments to each other. The community should issue a clear call to have this man as its priest; the priest should agree to live first as a brother to the brothers and sisters of the community and then, secondly, as a priest who comes to serve their priestly needs. The time, money, and accommodations of the priests should be more the responsibility of the community, both in helping determine how the priests should work and in making sure that they have sufficient support and time for refreshment. The prayer life of the priests needs to be shared more in the prayer life of the people. This will both help the people and insure that the priest continues to grow spiritually.

As for Matrimony, the gifts and needs of the married couple need to be evaluated. Other people in the community can take care of some needs of the married couple. Not every husband is a handyman, not every wife is a seamstress, not every couple is spiritually mature enough to give the right spiritual formation to their children. But within a community all these gifts are available.

The priest is called upon to do many things for which he is inadequately gifted or prepared. Not every priest is a music leader, a teacher, a leader of teenagers, a wise counselor of the elderly, a fund raiser, and an administrator. In the realm of spiritual gifts, some have gifts in prophecy, some in healing, some in evangelizing, and some in counseling. The priest needs to use the gifts he has and defer to other people in areas where others have the gifts. The priest needs to be less a jack-of-all-trades and more a coordinator of ministries. He needs to find the leaders and those with spiritual gifts and to spend time building them up. He needs to share his ministry broadly.

The rites of these sacraments should reflect these truths. The rite of Matrimony needs to have community participation. We have witnessed two weddings recently at The College of Steubenville in which the couples committed themselves to live and serve as part of the local Christian community. The representatives of the community spoke for the community in committing support, and at one point everyone gathered around the couple and prayed over them. During the prayer at one wedding, the father of the groom spoke in prophecy concerning the Lord's blessing on his son and daughter-in-law. At the engagement liturgy of the other couple, the father of the groom gave a similar prophecy. At the end of both weddings, it was clear to all present that we were deeply involved in supporting another marriage. We have noticed how ready the members of the community are to share in the concern for the children when they have been part of the baby's Baptism or the parents' marriage. The Word of God, a Christian community in Ann Arbor, Michigan, also gives this communal commitment and support of marriages, and there has not been a divorce in the seven years of community life. The community has approximately 1500 members.

The priest, at his ordination, is put in a new order of relationships with the people. In Halifax, Nova Scotia, the whole diocese once prepared for the ordination of three seminarians as deacons. The diocese fasted and held special prayer services during the evenings before ordination. The whole diocese was part of the ordination and everyone was invited to the reception following. Because of the publicity, all of the diocese was familiar with the names of the men they were supporting in prayer. When a priest came to a local parish in that diocese, he could expect to start with a better foundation. Much more needs to be changed and developed in this direction of communal involvement.

Another common quality and a problem in both sacraments is the call to fidelity:

-We need to see that fidelity to one wife was a sign of holiness in the early Church. When Jesus first taught this fidelity, Peter remarked that it was a hard saying, for under the Old Law a man need not be confined to one woman.

-In the Sacrament of Orders, after the fourth century, the Roman Church made celibacy a universal discipline. This required a fidelity which needed a spiritual base.

These realities emphasize the living faith needed for both Matrimony and priesthood. But, how do we draw on and grow in such faith? Both sacraments impart a permanent charism of the Spirit. Just as Baptism and Confirmation bring a presence of the Spirit which enables a person to draw on those graces necessary to begin a Christian life, so do Matrimony and Orders give those receiving them the graces needed to make their marriage or their priesthood work as it should. Married people and priests need to be taught to claim those graces in their daily lives.

Married persons can pray a simple prayer such as, "O Lord, I believe you are part of this marriage, that you are pledged to give us all the spiritual power we need for this marriage to be successful. So I claim that grace now in this present difficulty." It is preferable for the couple to pray together and to ask for a new sense of power, peace, and joy. Some compare this prayer to being baptized in the Spirit and also to receiving the sacrament of Matrimony again. This experience is common on Marriage Encounter Weekends, a program to teach couples to rediscover the power of the sacrament.

In a similar way, priests can draw on the power of the sacrament of Orders. One beautiful illustration of this is found in

Karl Rahner's meditation urging priests to renew their ordination. He holds that the permanent priestly character and the presence of the Holy Spirit as part of the priesthood make it possible for the priest to receive daily even a much greater fullness of the Spirit than on his ordination day. I (Fr. M.) have been with priests who decided to do this, laying hands on one another and renewing their ordination. As priests we were awed by the sense of new hope and new power.

The final paragraph of Rahner's meditation reads:

> Such personal new beginnings are therefore no romantic dream which in a festive hour forgets what we have experienced, how we have failed, what we have suffered and what we have become since our priestly ordination; they are no flight into illusion. No, we summon up the whole of our past life into this hour and add the unknown, dark future to it, and yet say our yes which gathers together everything past and to come in order to give it to God, so that he may make it a priestly life. No matter what has already happened in our life, deep down everything is still open and can still be fashioned into a priestly existence.*

Thus, for Matrimony and Orders, we are urging both a broadened communal concept and a deeper dependence on the actual graces of the sacraments. These sacraments will be alive in a fuller way if the community is involved and present and knows that this is a beginning of a new life together, and if the individuals receiving the sacraments expect and depend on the graces to meet their needs.

There is one further and most essential point. As we see the function of these sacraments to order new relationships, we become more conscious that the recipients need to be free

*Karl Rahner, Retreat for Priests, private notes.

from impediments from bad relationships in the past. Our experience has been that when the persons involved are able in faith to open themselves to the Lord's healing love, these impediments can be removed. Then they are free to receive the full power and grace of the sacrament. No longer is the sacrament a ritual they prepare for, but an opportunity for a new and deeply personal encounter with their God.

The couple preparing for marriage should ideally be able to find counsel, prayer, and healing through the one responsible for their pre-marital preparation. They should be prayed with individually for past wounds in relationships with other persons. The woman may feel guilty about a past sexual experience with another man. The young man may be fearful that he will be betrayed as he was by a woman he formerly knew. The kinds of past hurts are numerous, and unless the man and woman receive the Lord's healing love, they will enter marriage with barriers to full trust and union with another. The man and woman also need to be prayed with individually for past difficulties with their parents. Otherwise these hurts can carry over into their own parental relationships with their children, scarring and damaging them. They may also fear that their marriage could turn out as badly as their parents'; they *need* to know personally new freedom and peace from these fears and wounds. Otherwise, their marriage will begin on a very shaky foundation indeed! God desires their healing even more than they do, so that their marriage—the couple's covenant of fidelity and love for one another—can be a sign to the community of God's tender faithfulness to his people.

During the individual prayer for healing, the one *not* being prayed with should ideally be participating in the prayer and offering support by his or her presence. The person ministering should then pray over the *couple,* asking for God's healing love to enter any area of their relationship damaged by pain or guilt while they were dating and during the engagement period.

If the minister and the couple expect the Lord's healing love in all these areas, the man and woman will experience it. Then their marriage will truly be a whole and holy encounter with one another and with their God.

A similar preparation is needed for ordination to the priesthood. The priest will be called into a relationship of obedience and service to his bishop. He will be called to use authority in pastoring the people of his parish. As a preparation for priesthood, the one so called needs to be freed from the scars of bad relationships with authority figures such as his father, a former pastor, or his rector. Only then will he be free to serve under authority and to exercise it as the Lord directs. Too many priests have trouble today with their bishop, pastor, or dominating persons in the parish because they still carry resentments against earlier authority figures in their lives. God wants to heal that! When a man can open his heart and stop carrying those resentments in a self-righteous way, when he can forgive from his heart, he will know a new freedom in loving those very people. He will begin to know power as Jesus did: to forgive readily and live in free submission to his Father's will.

When he begins to experience God's healing love in all the past wounds of his personal life,

-he becomes free to be a humble servant; to wash feet in the spirit of Jesus

-from this position of freedom a new understanding of authority emerges. The priest is free to not cling to titles or positions of leadership but rather to serve in a way which enables the gifts of his people and his own gifts to be best used together for the upbuilding of one another and the glory of the Father.

-in this freedom the heart becomes pastoral. The priest is free to be loving, tender, strong, and faithful to his people. This is the way God calls him to be.

We pray that no one called to marriage or the priesthood will refuse the healing grace of this kind of prayer. As we indicated in the chapter on Anointing, God is love and so he always desires to do the most loving thing in our lives. Let us encourage one another to respond in faith to that gift of grace.*

What a realistic transformation would occur in society through marriages that were stable and joyful even in the midst of trial; what changes would take place in a Church which had healed and healing priests as its ministers. Such transformation is possible through community life and the power flowing from these sacraments. We have seen it and we believe.

We should not end the commentary on these sacraments without acknowledging questions implicit in our reflections. How will we develop a system of community selection of those to be priests and community commitment to support its

*There are many ways to pray for inner healing. The important element is to open to the healing love of Jesus to touch us in the wounded areas of our human spirit. This is usually done by accepting the love of Jesus for us, and therefore accepting ourselves as lovable within the context and scene of the harmful memories of our lives. One way in which this effectively happens is by what can be called extending the baptism of the Spirit. Those who have known the release of the Spirit in their lives have opened themselves to the love of Jesus and the pouring out of his spiritual gifts. Usually, however, there are areas of hurt within each person which are not open to this love at the time of the initial release of the Spirit. At a later time when these areas are recognized and we decide to let the Lord heal them with his love, what we do is open those new sectors of our inner life to the further release of the Spirit. If these areas are small and of minor importance, the healing experience will be of a minor nature. But if the areas are extensive and the hurt involved is serious, then the experience of the healing may be more freeing and more powerful than the experience of the initial release of the Spirit. The areas we have discussed in relation to Matrimony and Orders are usually important areas that respond in a powerful way to healing.

priests? Won't this mean a radical reevaluation of our seminary system? Won't we have to screen out seminarians who lack the qualities to lead a parish community? Won't we have to establish new norms on which priests will serve which parishes? And what about those permanent deacons? Shouldn't they be primarily servants of the people in a different way than priests and bishops? And what about the bishop? Won't similar standards of being called forth by priests and people as well as other bishops be necessary? And shouldn't bishops serve the people who called them forth? Finally, what about the ordinary offices of reader, acolyte, and the special office of exorcist, which are not part of the sacrament of Orders but are ministries directly related to it? Shouldn't there be modes of selecting and training men and women for these positions?

And looking at marriages, won't the parish priests have to include many members of the parish in the counseling and preparation of those contemplating marriage? Won't the marriage ceremony have to include some commitment by the parish? How about all those marriages entered into without an understanding of the sacrament, without an intent for total and permanent commitment, and without discernment and counseling on the rightness of the decision? What can be done about these marriages? And finally, shouldn't we know that there is a capacity for permanent love between husbands and wives before they enter a marriage which is indissoluble?

We now have acknowledged the questions. These are questions we believe all in the Church must face and to which we must respond. If such questions have a frustrating effect, reflect again on Chapter 2 and ponder how much the Church must come alive to make these sacraments be what they are called to be.

Epilogue

"...And Their Eyes Were Opened"

Now while he was with them at table, he took the bread
and said the blessing; then he broke it and handed it to
them. AND THEIR EYES WERE OPENED and they
recognized him; but he had vanished from their sight.

(Luke 24:30-31, Jerusalem Bible)

The message of this book is that the renewal of the sacraments depends on encountering Jesus in a decisive, dynamic
way in each sacrament. This will not come about primarily
through scholarly research on the history of the sacraments,
though that is important. This will not come about primarily
through more intense education on the standard catechesis of
the sacraments. This will not come about primarily through
better utilization of symbols or better wording of rites, better
music or better planning of liturgical celebrations, though
these are important. This will not *even* come about primarily
through well-organized homilies which correctly apply the
teachings of Scripture. Encountering Jesus comes about when
our eyes are opened to recognize Jesus in the sacraments and
when we decide to open our lives to a decisive encounter with
him there. In order to recognize Jesus in the sacraments we
must first of all know him in a personal way in our individual
lives through the power of the Spirit; then we must know him
as present in the sacrament of his Church. Once we have this

awareness, we are ready to see him in the sacramental actions. Once our eyes open to see him there, we can encounter him and let him transform our lives through his saving power. The actions by which this encounter takes place and develops are the actions of the sacramental rites. The pastoral proposals of this book are proposals for living out this encounter in each sacrament. Therefore we pray that, moved by the loving grace of the Lord, each of us may have our eyes opened to see Jesus and to meet him continually in his Church and through his Church in those special moments of encounter in the sacraments.

Appendix

We have made numerous references in this book to the power of the Spirit. We have done so because God's life and the power flowing from his Spirit are fundamental not merely for the way we perceive the sacraments but, in truth, for the way we view the whole Christian life.

For those who may question the importance of this concept or for those who desire a deeper understanding of what we mean by life in the Spirit, we offer the following explanation.

We believe by faith and through our personal experience in the past five or six years in the charismatic renewal that Jesus' promise not to leave us orphans is fulfilled as he told us;

-that through a faith-filled openness, God has released his Spirit in our lives so that we might know his continual presence and power to encourage, support, and upbuild one another in the Christian life;

-that such mutual support is possible through the love, joy, peace, patience, kindness, and all other fruits of the Spirit which grow in our lives to the extent we are open to receive them;

-that we are called to a continual openness to receive those *gifts* of his Spirit according to his plan and not ours; that we become vessels and servants of his life in us;

-that because of his Spirit and through those who are open to surrender their lives to his action, we are able to do even greater works than Jesus (John 14:12);

-that we are able to proclaim with our very lives "the kingdom of God is at hand" and see, as he promised, the lame cured, the blind see, the lepers cleansed and the poor having the gospel preached to them.

This is the good news in our lives—we know it and proclaim it. More deeply, we know it is meant for all Christians who have been baptized into his life. Those who fully surrender will know his power and life within them as they have never known it before. That life and wisdom will enable us all to face the problems of our lives, our relationships, our work, our society and world with the faith that can move mountains.

We are a people not meant to simply maintain the status quo, plug dikes, and tolerate situations with as much peace as we can muster.

By the death and resurrection of Jesus and our baptism into that life, we are a people of victory; a people who are enabled by God's Spirit and empowered by his gifts to proclaim that his kingdom is at hand with the power to transform the world.

Some may reject this as an unattainable ideal or as a pipe dream. But we have experienced its truth in our lives and in the lives of those gathered with us.

This is not to say we do not struggle, make mistakes, fail, and fall. But we believe, and our belief in a God ever-present to us empowers us to seek, to search, to struggle, and to know in the midst of our struggle a peace which surpasses all understanding.

The gifts of the Spirit as outlined in Paul's letter to the Corinthians (Chapters 12-14) are given not to set us apart, not to create an elite, not to separate us, but to unite and enable us to give mutual support. The gifts are given to the whole body—not all gifts to one person—because the gifts are *for* the body, not for an individual. They are given to each according to God's plan and our faith to receive. They are given to be used with the body of believers.

The gifts are for service. They are within our control in the sense that the Spirit is a God of order and peace, but we are also servants and the gifts are at his disposal to call forth in power when and where he wills.

When the gifts are exercised and their fruits manifested, men and women begin to realize more and more completely their interdependence. So does God desire that it be, "That they may be one even as we are one."

And so we desire to live and work and worship together since in this way we more fully know his power and direction for our personal lives, for us as a body and for the society in which we live.

We believe this to be God's plan: not to create a ghetto society but to live a communal life which in fact heals the rejection, alienation, and isolation of our present society, a life which enables those so healed to reach out with the wisdom of God to touch those who have not yet heard or been able to hear the good news, to strengthen the trembling hands and weak knees, and to be a light by which the world's problems may be understood and solved in the divine plan.

Bibliography

Of Theological Importance

Abbott, Walter M. (ed.). *The Documents of Vatican II*. New York: Guild Press, 1966.

Bro, Bernard, O.P. *The Spirituality of the Sacraments: Doctrine and Practice for Today*. Theodore DuBois (trans.). New York: Sheed and Ward, 1968.

Brown, Raymond E., S.S. [et. al.] (eds.). "Definition of Myth," *The Jerome Biblical Commentary*. Englewood Cliffs: Prentice-Hall, 1968, p. 740-1.

Cooke, Bernard J. *Christian Sacraments and Christian Personality*. New York: Holt, Rinehart and Winston, 1965.

Dillenschneider, Clement. *The Dynamic Power of Our Sacraments*. Sister M. Renelle (trans.). St. Louis: Herder Book Co., 1966.

Flannery, Austin, O.P. (ed.). *Vatican Council II: The Conciliar and Post Conciliar Documents*. Collegeville: The Liturgical Press, 1975.

McManus, Frederick R. *Sacramental Liturgy*. New York: Herder and Herder, 1967.

Poschmann, Bernhard. *Penance and the Anointing of the Sick*. Montreal: Palm Publishers, 1964.

Rahner, Karl. *The Church and the Sacraments*. New York: Herder and Herder, 1963.

Rahner, Karl (ed.). *Sacramentum Mundi*. Volumes 1-5. New York: Herder and Herder, 1968.

Schillebeeckx, Edward. *Christ the Sacrament of the Encounter with God*. Paul Barrett (trans.). New York: Sheed and Ward, 1963.

Smith, Richard F., S.J. "Inspiration and Inerrancy," Raymond E. Brown, S.S. [et. al.] (eds.). *The Jerome Biblical Commentary*. Englewood Cliffs: Prentice-Hall, Inc., 1968.

Of Special Pastoral Value

Evely, Louis. *Love Your Neighbor*. Imelda L'Italien (trans.). New York: Herder and Herder, 1969.

Ghezzi, Bert. *Build With the Lord*. Ann Arbor: Word of Life, 1976.

MacNutt, Francis, O.P. *Healing*. Notre Dame: Ave Maria Press, 1974.

Martin, George. *Reading Scripture as the Word of God*. Ann Arbor: Word of Life, 1975.

Mork, Dom Wulstan. *Led By the Spirit. A Primer of Sacramental Theology*. Milwaukee: Bruce Publishing Company, 1965.

Scanlan, Michael, T.O.R. *The Power in Penance: Confession and the Holy Spirit*. Notre Dame: Ave Maria Press, 1972.

Scanlan, Michael, T.O.R. *Inner Healing*. New York: Paulist Press, 1974.

Rite of Anointing and Pastoral Care of the Sick. Provisional text prepared by the International Commission on English in the Liturgy. New York: Pueblo Publishing Company, Inc., 1974.

Rite of Baptism for Children. United States Catholic Conference: Washington, D.C., 1969.

Rite of Christian Initiation of Adults. United States Catholic Conference. Washington, D.C., 1974.

Rite of Confirmation. Provisional Text. NCCB. Bishop's Committee on the Liturgy. Washington, D.C., 1972.

Rite of Funerals. United States Catholic Conference. Washington, D.C., 1971.

Rite of Marriage. United States Catholic Conference. Washington, D.C., 1969.

Rite of Penance. United States Catholic Conference. Washington, D.C., 1975.

The New Rite of Penance. Pevely: Federation of Diocesan Liturgical Commissions, 1974.